edTPA

Special Education Study Guide 2024-2025

- 📓 **Mastering Your Study Plan**: Learn how to create a personalized study strategy that suits your unique needs, maximizing efficiency and reducing wasted time.
- 🧠 **Enhancing Cognitive Performance**: Explore effective techniques to improve memory, deepen understanding, and solidify knowledge for long-term retention.
- ⏰ **Achieving Balance**: Apply smart time management methods to maintain a balance between study, work, and personal life, fostering a sustainable and healthy routine.
- 🎤 **Managing Stress Effectively**: Overcome exam anxiety with mindfulness, relaxation techniques, and resilience-building exercises to stay calm and focused when it matters most.
- ⬛ **Practicing for Success**: Understand the value of practice exams, sample questions, and mock tests, and learn how to analyze your performance to identify areas for growth.

Disclaimer of Liability:

This book is intended to provide readers with general information on various topics discussed within its content. It is sold with the understanding that neither the author nor the publisher is offering professional advice, including but not limited to legal, medical, or other specialized fields. Readers should seek the services of qualified professionals when professional assistance is needed.

Despite diligent efforts to ensure accuracy, errors or inaccuracies may be present. The author and publisher disclaim any liability for any loss or damage, whether direct or indirect, that may result from the use or reliance on the information in this book. This includes any potential loss or harm arising from the content provided.

The information in this book is provided "as is," without any warranties regarding its completeness, accuracy, usefulness, or timeliness. Readers are encouraged to consult certified experts or professionals for the most current and reliable information.

The viewpoints expressed in this book do not represent those of any specific organization or professional entity. Any perceived offenses towards individuals or groups are entirely unintentional.

TABLE OF CONTENT

STUDY GUIDE

Chapter 1: Understanding edTPA for Special Education
What is edTPA?
Key Components of edTPA in Special Education
The Role of Performance Assessment
Understanding the Rubrics and Scoring Criteria

Chapter 2: Planning for Instruction
Developing Instructional Objectives
Designing Effective Lesson Plans
Creating Adaptations and Modifications for Diverse Learners
Aligning Instruction with IEP Goals
Case Study: Planning for a Specific Student

Chapter 3: Creating and Utilizing Assessments
Types of Assessments (Formative and Summative)
Designing Assessments for Students with Special Needs
Collecting and Analyzing Data
Using Assessment Data to Inform Instruction
Case Study: Assessment and Adaptation

Chapter 4: Implementing Instruction
Strategies for Effective Instruction
Managing Classroom Behavior and Engagement
Differentiating Instruction for Diverse Learners
Effective Use of Educational Technology
Case Study: Implementing a Lesson

Chapter 5: Analyzing Teaching and Learning
Reflecting on Teaching Practice
Analyzing Student Learning Outcomes
Identifying Strengths and Areas for Improvement
Using Feedback to Improve Practice
Case Study: Reflective Practice and Improvement

Chapter 6: Building Positive Relationships
Establishing Relationships with Students
Collaborating with Families and Other Professionals
Building a Supportive Learning Environment
Addressing Cultural and Linguistic Diversity
Case Study: Building and Maintaining Relationships

Understanding edTPA for Special Education in Chapter One

A key element of teacher certification is the edTPA (Teacher Performance Assessment), which assesses prospective teachers' knowledge and practical abilities. Comprehending the subtleties of the edTPA is crucial for individuals seeking certification in Special Education. This chapter gives a thorough introduction to the edTPA, emphasizing its applicability to special education, the format of the test, and the scoring standards.

edTPA: What is it?

The purpose of the performance-based edTPA is to assess a candidate's readiness to teach, plan, and monitor student learning. To make sure that teacher candidates are ready for the demands of the classroom, some states in the United States use the edTPA, which was developed by the Stanford Center for Assessment, Learning, and Equity (SCALE). In contrast to conventional exams that emphasize academic knowledge, the edTPA demands applicants to use real-world classroom experience to illustrate their teaching abilities.

The special needs of kids with disabilities are taken into account in the edTPA's standards for Special Education. This entails developing individualized education programs (IEPs), adapting instruction to meet the requirements of students with varying learning disabilities, and evaluating student progress in ways that take into account their difficulties.

Important edTPA Elements for Special Education

The following are the main elements of the edTPA for Special Education:

Developing Lesson Plans and Assessments that Meet the Needs of All Students, Including Those with Disabilities: This component centers on how successfully candidates create lesson plans and assessments. The capacity to set goals, choose teaching resources, and organize accommodations and changes must be shown by candidates.

Teaching and Instructing Students: This area evaluates how well candidates carry out their lesson plans and involve students in the educational process. It entails watching candidates in action while they instruct, observing how successfully they employ instructional strategies, control classroom behavior, and modify their lessons in response to feedback from students.

Examining Student Learning: Applicants must demonstrate how they employ assessments to gauge the progress of their students and modify their curriculum as necessary. This entails creating tests that are suitable for students with impairments, evaluating test results, and applying the knowledge gained to guide instruction in the future.

Thinking Back on Teaching: An essential component of edTPA is reflection. Candidates must assess the efficacy of their instruction, examine their own teaching methods, and pinpoint areas in need of development. This entails considering the effects of instructional decisions as well as the learning outcomes of students.

The Function of Performance Evaluation

Performance evaluation, as demonstrated by edTPA, places more emphasis on the real-world application of teaching techniques than it does on abstract concepts. This requires candidates for special education to show that they can modify their curriculum to fit the requirements of kids with a variety of disabilities. In order to evaluate performance, candidates must:

Plan Meaningful Instruction: Well-thought-out planning includes establishing precise goals, creating stimulating exercises, and making modifications. In the context of special education, this also entails making sure that all children have access to the resources and activities and coordinating instruction with IEP goals.

Effectively Implement Instruction: To satisfy a range of learning needs, a number of instructional methodologies must be used. The capacity to control classroom dynamics, offer tailored support, and uphold a supportive learning environment are requirements for candidates.

Evaluate and Consider Student Learning: In order to comprehend student development and modify education, effective evaluation procedures are essential. Candidates who want to improve student learning must gather and evaluate data, offer insightful criticism, and consider how they teach.

Recognizing the Scoring Standards and Rubrics

A series of rubrics that offer comprehensive standards for assessing applicant performance are used to assign scores for the edTPA. Each evaluation component is evaluated in accordance with predetermined criteria, and scores are given according to the caliber of the supporting documentation. The Special Education rubrics highlight the following:

Alignment with Standards: Applicants must demonstrate how their lesson plans and evaluations meet both IEP objectives and state standards. This entails stating learning objectives precisely and illustrating how instructional activities meet these objectives.

Effectiveness of Instruction: The candidates' execution of their lesson plans, including their use of teaching methodologies, classroom management tactics, and accommodations for students with disabilities, is assessed using the rubrics.

Use of Assessment Data: Candidates' abilities to gather and evaluate assessment data, decide on instruction with knowledge, and offer constructive criticism to students are evaluated.

Reflective Practice: Constant progress in teaching requires the capacity to reflect on one's methods. Applicants must show that they can assess student learning results, review their own instruction, and pinpoint areas in which they still need to improve.

Getting Ready for Special Education's edTPA

A deliberate approach is needed to prepare for edTPA, which involves practicing reflective analysis, creating solid lesson plans, and comprehending the assessment components. The following advice can help you prepare effectively:

Get Acquainted with the Rubrics: Go over the edTPA rubrics thoroughly to comprehend the scoring requirements. This will assist you in staying on task and guarantee that your submissions adhere to the necessary requirements.

Contemplate Carefully: Create comprehensive lesson plans and evaluations that cater to the requirements of every student, including those with special needs. When making your strategy, think about how you will meet the requirements and learning styles of various students.

Practice Teaching and Reflecting: Get experience by instructing students in a variety of classroom environments and engaging in reflective practice. Make use of mentor and colleague comments to refine your instruction and develop your reflective abilities.

Collect Proof Methodically: Gather documentation of your instruction, such as lesson plans, examples of student work, and assessment results. Sort this data so that it directly responds to the edTPA rubrics.

Seek Assistance: To assist you in getting ready, make use of tools like study guides, practice questions, and mentorship. Participate in workshops or study groups to get more perspectives and input.

Chapter 2: Organizing Instruction

Precise planning is the first step towards effective Special Education instruction. Creating lessons and activities that cater to the various needs of students—especially those with disabilities—is a crucial aspect of lesson planning. The fundamentals of lesson planning, assessment design, instructional objectives development, lesson plan creation, and meeting the special needs of students with disabilities are all covered in this chapter.

Formulating Educational Goals

The foundation of a successful teaching strategy is the instructional objectives. They provide students specific expectations for what they should know and be able to do at the conclusion of a course or unit. Developing these objectives for Special Education necessitates a thorough comprehension of the unique needs and talents of each student. Here's how to create goals that have meaning:

Ensure that your goals are in line with any applicable state or federal criteria. This frequently entails incorporating goals from the Individualized Education Program (IEP) into your lesson planning for Special Education.

Be quantifiable and Specific: In order to facilitate efficient evaluation, objectives must be both quantifiable and specific. For instance, state clearly that "students will be able to identify and write 10 high-frequency sight words" as opposed to aiming to "improve reading skills," which is too general.

Take Students' demands into Account: Adapt your goals to meet the various demands of your students. This could entail establishing several goals for various children according to their skills, difficulties, and IEP needs.

Make sure your goals are Time-bound, Relevant, Specific, Measurable, and Achievable by applying the SMART criteria. With the use of this framework, learning objectives can be made more achievable and practical within the allotted time.

Creating Powerful Lesson Plans

To ensure that learning objectives are accomplished and to guide instruction, a well-structured lesson plan is essential. Lesson plans for Special Education must incorporate techniques for adjustments and differentiation. Here's how to draft a lesson plan that works:

A clear introduction, instructions, guided practice, autonomous practice, and a conclusion should all be included in the lesson structure. Every element ought to be planned to fulfill the goals and cater to the various needs of the students.

Choose the Right Materials: Make sure that all students have access to and enjoyment from the materials and resources you choose. This could entail the use of assistive technology, visual aids, or modified texts for students with disabilities.

Include Differentiation: Make sure to include opportunities for students to interact with the material, demonstrate their comprehension, and get help in a variety of ways. This can involve changing the assignments, utilizing different teaching strategies, and providing extra materials.

Include techniques to adapt and change instruction in accordance with students' IEPs in your plan for accommodations and modifications. You may, for instance, give projects more time, use simpler terminology, or offer one-on-one assistance.

Get Ready for Emotional and Behavioral Support: Consider and prepare for any behavioral or emotional requirements. To assist children' emotional health and classroom performance, use techniques like behavior charts, personalized check-ins, and positive reinforcement.

Formulating Evaluations for Diverse Students
Assessments are essential for monitoring student development and directing instruction. Assessments for Special Education must be created in a way that fairly represents the knowledge and skills of every student. Here's how to properly design and administer assessments:

Create Assessments That Are in Line with Goals: Make sure that the assessments are in line with the learning objectives. Assessments for Special Education should gauge the particular objectives listed in each student's Individualized Education Plan (IEP).

Incorporate a Range of Assessment Types: To evaluate students' learning, combine formative and summative evaluations. Summative assessments, like examinations and projects, measure overall performance, whereas formative assessments, like quizzes and class discussions, offer continuous feedback.

Assessors should be modified as needed to accommodate students with disabilities. This could entail making examinations accessible and equitable as well as offering alternate formats, including oral exams or visual aids.

Analyze Assessment Data: To measure student progress and modify instruction, gather and examine assessment data. To determine a student's areas of strength and areas that require improvement, look for patterns in their performance.

Give Students Meaningful Feedback: Give students helpful criticism that points them in the direction of progress. In order to help students in Special Education understand their progress and areas for improvement, feedback should be precise, actionable, and easy to grasp.

Matching Instruction to IEP Objectives
To make sure that the educational requirements of students with disabilities are satisfied, it is crucial to match instruction with their IEP goals. To incorporate IEP goals into your preparation, follow these steps:

Examine IEPs Completely: Learn about the objectives, adjustments, and accommodations listed in each student's IEP. Make use of this knowledge to guide your teaching tactics and lesson planning.

Establish Relevant Goals: Make sure your lesson plans reflect the objectives listed in each student's IEP. This guarantees that your instruction meets each student's unique needs and advances them as a whole.

Incorporate Accommodations and changes: Make sure your lesson plans take into account the accommodations and changes outlined in the IEP. This could entail making adjustments to educational materials, offering more help, or utilizing assistive technology.

Continually assess student development and make necessary adjustments to your course based on how well the accommodations and changes work. Make the required modifications based on assessment results and comments to best serve the requirements of your pupils.

Case Study: Organizing for a Particular Learner
Take a look at this case study to see how the process of lesson planning is done:

Student Profile: Jamie is a fifth-grader with attention deficit hyperactivity disorder (ADHD) and a specific learning difficulty in reading. Jamie's IEP outlines objectives for enhancing comprehension of what he reads and creating attention-management techniques.
Learning Objectives:

Jamie will summarize the key points and illustrative features in a brief reading passage. Jamie will arrange his ideas and thoughts during reading activities using a graphic organizer.
Curriculum:

Introduction: Give a succinct synopsis of the reading material and establish specific goals for the class.
Instruction: To assist Jamie with organizing information, present a graphic organizer. Reading aloud from a passage while demonstrating how to use the organizer.
Guided Practice: Give Jamie a passage to read and assist him in identifying the major concepts and details using the visual organizer.
As an individual exercise, assign Jamie to finish a similar task in which she must arrange data from a fresh section using the graphic organizer.
Closure: Go over the key points and specifics mentioned in the class and offer your assessment of Jamie's usage of the graphic organizer.
Evaluation:
Formative: Track Jamie's involvement in guided practice and give prompt comments.
Summative: Evaluate Jamie's use of the graphic organizer and his capacity to recognize the key points and specifics in a piece of writing.
Allowances:

Give Jamie more time to finish his reading assignments.
Reduce distractions by working in a calm environment.

Chapter 3: Formulating and Applying Evaluations

Effective teaching is built around assessments, particularly in special education. They support instructional decisions, offer vital information about students' development, and assist in modifying training to fit a variety of requirements. The process of developing and applying assessments in Special Education is examined in this chapter, with a focus on the significance of producing efficient tests, evaluating data, and utilizing the findings to guide instruction.

Assessment Types

It is essential to comprehend the various assessment formats in order to measure student learning effectively. Assessments in Special Education should be made to take into account a variety of skill levels and give precise information about each student's development.

Formative assessments are continuous evaluations carried out in the course of teaching. They support instructional modifications and provide as a means of tracking student comprehension. Exams, class discussions, and casual observations are a few examples. Formative evaluations are used to direct daily education and offer prompt feedback.

Summative Evaluations: These tests measure students' knowledge at the conclusion of a lesson. These are usually more formal and extensive, including standardized assessments, projects, or final exams. Summative exams used in Special Education should be modified to ensure that student achievement is appropriately measured in relation to each student's unique goals.

Diagnostic tests: These tests are used to determine pupils' strengths, weaknesses, and individual requirements prior to the start of education. Diagnostic tests support the development of effective interventions and the customization of instruction to each student's needs.

Dynamic assessments: These go beyond a student's present performance level to consider their potential for learning. Dynamic evaluations frequently entail interactive exercises in which students are evaluated on their ability to acquire new concepts and receive feedback and assistance along the way.

Creating Efficient Evaluations

Several important factors must be taken into account when creating tests that effectively reflect student learning, especially for children with disabilities. Validity, reliability, and alignment with learning objectives are key components of effective assessments.

Align with Instructional Objectives: Make sure that the goals outlined in lesson plans are precisely met by the evaluations. This entails matching evaluations to particular learning objectives and IEP goals in the context of special education.

Think About Accessibility: Create tests that are usable by all students, including those with impairments. This may be utilizing other forms (big print, audio versions, etc.) or offering extra help (longer hours, one-on-one help, etc.).

Include Several Formats: To accommodate varying learning styles and capacities, employ a range of assessment formats. Written exams, spoken presentations, hands-on demonstrations, and graphic projects can all fall under this category. Giving pupils a variety of methods to show what they understand can help paint a more complete picture of their skills.

Assure Fairness and Clarity: Evaluations must to be precise and unambiguous. Make sure the evaluation is equitable for every student and that the directions are clear. Steer clear of words or information that could harm pupils who have special educational needs.

Construct Rubrics and Scoring Criteria: Draft comprehensive rubrics that delineate the requirements for triumphant performance. Rubrics aid in the consistent and objective grading process and provide students with lucid feedback on their areas of strength and growth.

Making Use of Assessment Data
After exams are completed, it's crucial to analyze and make use of the results in order to inform education and foster student development. Using assessment data effectively requires a few crucial steps:

Collect and Arrange Data: Compile evaluation findings in a methodical manner and arrange them for straightforward analysis. This could entail tracking performance over time with spreadsheets or evaluation software.

Evaluate Student Performance: Look over the information to find trends and patterns in the students' performance. Identify the areas in which pupils succeed and the ones in which they falter. Take into account how disabled students perform in relation to their goals and accommodations when implementing special education programs.

Utilize Data to Inform Instruction: Modify your teaching tactics based on the conclusions drawn from data analysis. For instance, you might need to go over a subject again and offer more assistance if a sizable portion of the class is having trouble understanding it.

Differentiate your instruction by adjusting it to each student's requirements based on evaluation results. This could entail adjusting assignments, offering more resources, or providing other ways for students with impairments to interact with the material.

Give Students Targeted Feedback: Based on their performance on the evaluation, provide students with detailed and useful feedback. Feedback need to be constructive, with the goal of assisting pupils in realizing their strengths and areas for development.

Track Student development: Analyze student development over time to determine how well interventions and instructional strategies are working. Frequent monitoring enables prompt modifications to education and helps guarantee that students are making sufficient progress toward their objectives.

Case Study: Creating and Applying Evaluations

Take a look at the following case study to see how the procedure works:

Student Profile: Alex struggles with reading comprehension and has autism spectrum disorder (ASD). He is a seventh-grader. Alex's IEP has objectives for using graphic organizers and increasing understanding.

Design of Assessment:

Formative Assessment: A reading comprehension quiz with both multiple-choice and short-answer questions given once a week. Alex intends to utilize a visual organizer to assist in organizing his answers.

Summative Assessment: a final reading comprehension exam with questions that call for in-depth explanations. Throughout the exam, Alex will have access to a graphic organizer. Gathering and Analyzing Data:

Compile and arrange test and quiz results to monitor Alex's progress over time. Examine the data to see trends, such as questions that Alex finds difficult or places where he may improve.

Making Use of Data

Adapt the curriculum in light of Alex's performance. Give him more practice and assistance in that area if he frequently has trouble answering a particular kind of question.

Provide specific criticism on Alex's use of the graphic organizer, emphasizing his strengths and areas for development.

Provide extra materials or adapted tasks to assist Alex's understanding needs in order to differentiate instruction.

Chapter 4: Putting Instruction into Practice

Effective instruction implementation is essential to good teaching, especially in special education, where serving a variety of needs necessitates the meticulous application of carefully thought-out solutions. The practical components of teaching are covered in this chapter, along with strategies for using technology, organizing the classroom, engaging students, and differentiating instruction. It also emphasizes methods for resolving issues and guaranteeing that every student has the chance to achieve.

Getting Students Involved: Good learning requires student engagement. Pupils who are actively involved in class are more likely to remember what they have learned and to meet their learning objectives. The following techniques aim to improve student involvement:

Establish an Inclusive Environment: Encourage a learning environment in which each and every student feels important and included. Celebrate different cultures, speak inclusively, and make sure that the resources and activities in your classroom represent the diversity of your pupils.

Employ Diverse Instructional Strategies: To accommodate a range of learning preferences, use a combination of instructional techniques. Direct education, practical exercises, group projects, and multimedia presentations are a few examples of this. For instance, whereas kinesthetic learners might be more engaged with hands-on exercises, visual learners might gain more from diagrams and films.

Connect the Content to Actual Events: To make learning more engaging and relevant, tie teachings to real-world situations. Use real-world examples and scenarios, for instance, that are relevant to the interests and experiences of your pupils.

Include Student attracts: Find out what attracts your pupils and include such topics in your classes. This can improve motivation and add enjoyment to the learning process. Use examples from math or science classes that pertain to animals, for instance, if a student has an interest in animals.

Employ Interactive Activities: To keep students engaged, use cooperative and interactive learning exercises. Peer education, group projects, and conversations can increase participation and offer chances for social contact.

Controlling the Classroom
Establishing a healthy learning environment in the classroom requires effective classroom management. Classroom management techniques in special education must be customized to meet each student's individual needs.

Define Clear Expectations: Clearly state what is expected of students' conduct and academic achievement on a regular basis. To help people remember rules and procedures, use visual aids like charts and posters. Make certain that all students get and comprehend the expectations in a clear and concise manner.

Create an organized Schedule: To offer stability and predictability, put in place an organized daily schedule. Regular schedules lessen anxiety and help children understand what to expect, especially those with autism spectrum disorders or other special needs.

Employ Positive Reinforcement: Give incentives, prizes, or other recognition for good deeds and accomplishments. Students that receive positive reinforcement are more likely to obey regulations, participate in class activities, and be motivated.

Deal With Behavioral Problems Early on: Put preventative measures into place and deal with behavioral problems before they get out of hand. Proactively assist kids who might have trouble controlling their behavior by implementing strategies like creating a behavior management plan or offering sensory breaks.

Give Step-by-Step Instructions and Support: Clearly and concisely describe tasks and activities. Use visual aids to aid in understanding and instruction compliance, such as checklists or schedules. Provide extra help as required, such as individualized support or redesigned assignments.

Instructional Differentiation
In Special Education, differentiation is essential to fulfilling the unique needs of students. You can guarantee that every student has the chance to succeed by adjusting instruction to meet their specific requirements.

Content and Material Modification: Adapt instructional materials and content to the skills and learning preferences of your students. This could entail making texts easier to read, utilizing larger fonts, or offering reading materials in alternate media, such audio versions.

Provide Flexible Grouping: Provide students a variety of possibilities for contact and collaboration by using flexible grouping tactics. To provide a variety of learning experiences, divide students into groups according to their ability levels, interests, or learning needs. Then, rotate the groups.

Offer a Variety of Learning Activities: To cater to varying learning styles, provide a variety of activities. For instance, to accommodate various learning styles, use written assignments, visual aids, and practical experiments.

Assessments should be modified to accommodate each person's needs. This can entail giving students more time, employing multiple forms, or conducting assessments in other ways, such projects or oral presentations.

Put Scaffolding into Practice: Offer scaffolding to assist students in finishing assignments. Tasks are scaffolded by dividing them into smaller, more achievable steps and offering assistance at each turn. As pupils become more self-reliant and confident, gradually cut down on the support.

Using Technology Technology can help meet a range of learning demands and improve instruction. The key to successfully integrating technology into your teaching is to choose the right tools and include them into your lessons.

Select Assistive Technology: Assist students with impairments by utilizing assistive technology resources. Screen readers, adaptable keyboards, and speech-to-text software are a few examples of this. Make sure the technological resources you use fit your kids' individual needs and are easily available.

Use Educational Apps and Software: To enhance learning and offer interactive experiences, make use of educational apps and software. Select apps that fit educational goals and are made for special education.

Employ Multimedia Resources: Incorporate online games, interactive simulations, and movies into your courses. Students with varying learning styles can be engaged and given a variety of learning experiences using multimedia.

Encourage Collaboration and Communication: Encourage student collaboration and communication by utilizing technology. Peer contact and group work can be facilitated by tools like video conferencing, collaborative papers, and online discussion forums.

Provide Students with Opportunities for Digital Learning: Give students the chance to use self-directed learning and explore digital learning tools. Students should be encouraged to use technology for projects, research, and creative expression.

Overcoming Obstacles
The problems of implementing instruction in special education are unique. Effectively addressing these obstacles requires foreseeing possible problems and creating contingency plans to deal with them.

Adapt to Specific Needs: Be ready to modify your pedagogical approaches in response to the unique requirements and reactions of each learner. Meeting the varied needs of kids with disabilities requires flexibility.

Seek Assistance and Resources: Make use of the assistance and resources provided by specialists, coworkers, and instructional materials. To improve your teaching methods, work together with other experts, like counselors and special education teachers.

Always Evaluate and Develop: Evaluate your teaching methods on a regular basis and get input from mentors, colleagues, and students. Make changes based on this feedback, and take care of any obstacles you face.

Keep Your Persistence and Patience: Working with students who have disabilities calls for perseverance and patience. Even in the face of difficulties, stay committed to your objectives and never stop offering assistance and motivation.

Chapter 5: Examining Instruction and Input

Effective instruction requires careful analysis of both teaching and learning, particularly in special education. In order to improve educational results, this process include assessing the effectiveness of teaching tactics, comprehending student progress, and making data-driven decisions. This chapter examines techniques for studying teaching and learning, such as evaluating the efficacy of instruction, deciphering data on student performance, and making adjustments in response to conclusions.

Evaluating the Effectiveness of Instruction
Assessing the efficacy of your pedagogical approaches facilitates the identification of whether learning objectives are being fulfilled and whether students are making the anticipated development. Several tactics are necessary for effective instruction assessment, including:

Self-Reflection: Consider your teaching methods on a regular basis. Think about inquiries like these: Were the learning goals met? Did the pupils interact with the subject matter? What elements of the lesson were successful, and what might be made better? Finding your teaching strengths and places for improvement is made easier with reflective practice.

Peer Observations: Ask your peers to watch you teach and offer helpful criticism. Peer observations provide an unbiased assessment of your teaching strategies and might point out areas that need work that you may not have noticed.

Student Input: Collect student input regarding their educational experiences. Utilize surveys, casual discussions, or feedback forms to gain insight into what your students find problematic or helpful in your classes.

Evaluation of Lesson Plans: Examine and evaluate your lesson plans on a regular basis. Make sure they incorporate appropriate differentiation and adjustments, are in line with instructional goals, and cater to a variety of learning needs.

Analyze the efficacy of the instructional tactics you use in order to evaluate them. Think about whether the tactics are assisting students in achieving the intended goals, promoting their learning, and capturing their attention.

Analyzing Data on Student Performance
Making educated judgments about education and assessing development depend on having a thorough understanding of student performance data. Here's how to properly evaluate and use this data:

Gather and Arrange Data: Gather information from several tests, such as formative, summative, and diagnostic tests, in a methodical manner. Use spreadsheets or assessment tools to arrange the data so that it can be easily analyzed.

Examine Patterns and Trends: Examine the data for patterns and trends. Determine the areas in which pupils are performing well and the ones in which they are not. To obtain a complete picture of a student's development, look for trends in evaluations over time and across many domains.

Disaggregate Data: To obtain insights into particular issues or triumphs, break down data by various student groupings, such as by learning needs or handicap category. Data disaggregation facilitates the discovery of trends that might be unique to particular student populations.

Compare Performance Against Goals: Evaluate how well students are doing in relation to the objectives and goals specified in their Individualized Education Programs (IEPs). Assess whether pupils are achieving their objectives and note any gaps that require filling.

Utilize Data to Determine Interventions: Determine any adjustments or interventions that may be required to assist student learning based on the analysis. This can entail making modifications to teaching tactics, offering more resources, or carrying out focused interventions.

Putting Improvements Into Practice
Improving instructional practices through the application of learning and teaching analytic insights is essential to improving student outcomes. Here's how to apply changes in an efficient manner:

Instructional Strategy Adjustment: Make adjustments to your teaching methods in light of feedback and data. For instance, if a certain idea is proving difficult for the pupils, think about implementing other teaching strategies or giving them more chances to practice.

Further Differentiation: Adapt differentiation tactics to better suit the requirements of individual students based on data on student performance. This could entail giving struggling students more assistance or giving advanced students more difficult assignments.

Update and revise lesson plans to accommodate any gaps or issues that are found. Make sure that lessons from the past are incorporated into future lesson plans so that they better assist students' learning.

Improved Resources and Support: Depending on the needs of the students, provide more resources or help. This can entail supplying extra materials, making use of assistive technology, or giving lessons in small groups or one-on-one coaching.

Monitor and Assess adjustments: Put the adjustments into practice and keep an eye on how they're affecting students' learning. Continue to assess the efficacy of the modifications and make any necessary additional adjustments.

Case Study: Examining Instruction and Instruction

Take a look at the following case study to see how teaching and learning analysis works:

Student Profile: Maria is a student in the eighth grade who has a particular type of math learning difficulty. Her IEP has objectives for strengthening her ability to solve problems and comprehend mathematical ideas.

Evaluation Information:

Formative Assessments: Classwork and weekly tests show that Maria has trouble solving word problems.

Summative Assessments: Maria's performance on the end-of-unit test indicates that she is not solving problems at the grade level.

Evaluation:

Find Patterns: Maria's persistent word problem difficulties point to a possible problem with understanding or applying mathematical principles.

Analyze performance data for other students who have comparable needs to determine whether Maria is the only one facing this difficulty or if it is a typical occurrence.

In comparison to the goals: Analyze Maria's progress in relation to her IEP's objectives for her ability to solve problems.

Enhancements:

Modify Instructional Strategies: Give students more practice with word problems and include explicit instruction on problem-solving techniques. To help with understanding, provide step-by-step instructions and visual aids.

Further Distinguish: Give Maria customized word puzzles and one-on-one assistance to help her with her unique difficulties. Utilize visual aids or manipulatives to aid with her conceptual understanding.

Edit Course Plans: Revise lesson plans to give students more targeted training on word problems and ways for solving them. Provide practice and review opportunities.

Boost Assistance and Materials: Provide extra resources to help with skill reinforcement, including interactive applications or practice worksheets. By using tutoring or small group instruction, give extra assistance.

Observe and Assess:

Analyze Maria's development with the updated tactics and tools. Utilize formative evaluations to monitor progress and make necessary instructional adjustments.

Chapter 6: Establishing Harmonious Connections

Especially in Special Education, developing strong relationships is essential to establishing a welcoming and productive learning environment. Trust, involvement, and collaboration are vital for student success and are fostered by positive connections between educators, students, families, and coworkers. This chapter looks at how to establish and nurture these connections, comprehend how they affect learning, and deal with any obstacles that may come up.

Recognizing the Value of Healthy Relationships
A fruitful and encouraging educational experience is built on positive relationships. They support:

Enhanced Student Engagement: Students are more likely to be interested in and driven to learn when they have a sense of connection to their teacher and peers. Good interactions provide students a sense of community and motivate them to participate fully in class.

Enhanced Academic Achievement: Pupils who enjoy a close rapport with their educators are more likely to succeed academically. A teacher's confidence and readiness to encourage their students can increase their willingness to take chances in the classroom.

Better Social and Behavior Skills: Strong bonds with others support the development of social and behavior skills. When students feel appreciated and understood, they are more inclined to abide by the rules and behave politely.

Good Relationships Promote Open Communication and Collaboration: Teachers, students, and families may work together more effectively when there are strong relationships between them. This cooperative strategy guarantees that all parties are assisting one another and striving toward shared objectives.

Developing Harmonious Connections with Students
Building solid, constructive relationships with kids requires a number of crucial behaviors, including:

Demonstrate Sincere Interest and Concern: Invest some time in getting to know each of your pupils personally. Find out about their problems, hobbies, and strengths. Taking a sincere interest in their life and welfare promotes rapport-building and trust.

Provide a Safe and Supportive Environment: Make your classroom a place where children feel supported and safe. Encourage kids with words and deeds, use positive reinforcement, and provide opportunity for them to express their emotions.

Be Fair and Consistent: Be fair in your interactions and expectations with pupils. Building trust and ensuring that students comprehend and adhere to classroom rules and procedures are two benefits of adopting a fair and open approach.

Promote Student Voice: Allow students to voice their ideas and make decisions regarding their education. Promoting student voice makes students feel important and engaged in their learning process.

Offer Tailored Support: Tailored support should be given according to the requirements of each learner. Adapt your teaching methods and modifications to each student's particular needs, and offer more help when required.

Developing Harmonious Partnerships with Families
In order to enhance student success, it is imperative that families participate in the educational process. Working effectively with families entails:

Create Open Communication: Have regular, honest communication channels with families. Provide parents with updates on their child's development and classroom activities via a variety of channels, including phone calls, emails, and newsletters.

Develop Empathy and Respect: Show empathy and respect in all of your encounters with families. Recognize and value the role that parents play in their children's education, and collaborate with them to resolve any issues or problems.

Engage Families in the Decision-Making Process: Involve families in significant choices concerning their child's education. This may be attending IEP meetings, talking about objectives and tactics, and getting their advice on how to best assist their child's education.

Offer Families Support and Resources: Give families the tools and resources they need to support their children at home. This can involve giving families access to local resources, conducting training sessions or workshops, and disseminating information on effective teaching methods.

Celebrate Achievements Together: Inform and honor students' families about their accomplishments. Acknowledging and applauding accomplishments strengthens a relationship and emphasizes the value of teamwork.

Developing Good Connections with Coworkers
Working together, educators can provide children the entire help they need. Developing a good rapport with coworkers entails:

Encourage Collaboration: Cooperate with other educators, experts, and support personnel. Exchange ideas, tactics, and materials to improve students' overall educational experience.

Respect and Encourage One Another: Be mindful of the experiences and viewpoints of your coworkers. Be receptive to criticism and ideas while providing assistance and inspiration.

Take Part in Professional Development: To improve your knowledge and abilities, take advantage of professional development programs. Work together with colleagues to implement fresh approaches and methods in the classroom.

Effective Communication: Keep lines of communication open and transparent with coworkers. Communicate frequently, talk about the development of the students, and work together to resolve any issues.

Create a Positive Team Culture: Make a constructive and encouraging contribution to the team culture. Celebrate victories, acknowledge one another's efforts, and cooperate to overcome obstacles.

Overcoming Obstacles in Relationship Development
Even though developing healthy relationships is important, problems can still occur. Effectively addressing these issues entails:

Constructive Conflict Resolution: When disagreements arise, address them with an attitude of problem-solving. To settle disputes and keep good relationships, communicate politely and look for common ground.

Acknowledging and Handling Bias: Recognize and address any prejudices that can influence how you engage with coworkers, families, or pupils. Examine your methods and look for assistance or training to help you confront and get rid of any biases.

Handling Stress and Burnout: Teaching may be difficult, particularly in the field of special education. Take action to reduce stress and avoid burnout by doing things like asking coworkers for help, taking care of yourself, and striking a healthy work-life balance.

Seeking Assistance and Resources: Consult mentors, managers, or professional associations for assistance if you continue to have trouble forming relationships. Make use of the tactics and resources at your disposal to strengthen your strategy and deal with any problems.

Case Study: Establishing Harmonious Connections
Take a look at the following case study to see how creating strong relationships might help:

Scenario: Ms. Johnson teaches special education and works with Liam, an ADHD kid. Liam has been having trouble with behavior and participation in the classroom despite her best attempts.

Techniques:

Interacting with Liam: Ms. Johnson makes an effort to find out about Liam's preferences and areas of interest. She finds out that he likes to sketch, so she adds drawing exercises to his courses to get students more involved.

Interacting with Liam's Family: Ms. Johnson sets up frequent correspondence with Liam's parents. She provides updates on Liam's development and talks about methods they might use at home to help his behavior.

Working Together: Ms. Johnson develops a behavior management plan for Liam in conjunction with the behavior expert and school counselor. They collaborate to put plans into action and keep an eye on Liam's development.

Honoring Achievements: Ms. Johnson and Liam's family honor all of his accomplishments, no matter how modest. Liam's motivation and self-assurance are increased by this encouraging affirmation.

Result: Through cultivating a good rapport with Liam, his family, and coworkers, Ms. Johnson is able to enhance Liam's participation and behavior in the classroom. All parties engaged guarantee Liam constant support and encouragement through the collaborative approach.

Practice Questions and Answers Explanations 2024-2025

1. Which of the following best describes a key characteristic of effective lesson planning for students with special needs?

A) Creating one-size-fits-all lesson plans
B) Ignoring individual learning goals
C) Incorporating individualized accommodations and modifications
D) Focusing only on academic content without considering student needs

Answer: C) Incorporating individualized accommodations and modifications

Explanation: Effective lesson planning for students with special needs involves incorporating individualized accommodations and modifications. This ensures that lessons are tailored to meet the unique needs of each student, providing them with the necessary support to access and engage with the curriculum.

2. What is the primary purpose of using formative assessments in a Special Education classroom?

A) To evaluate overall student progress at the end of the year
B) To measure the effectiveness of the entire instructional program
C) To provide ongoing feedback to adjust instruction and support student learning
D) To rank students based on their performance

Answer: C) To provide ongoing feedback to adjust instruction and support student learning

Explanation: Formative assessments are used to provide ongoing feedback that helps educators adjust their instruction and better support student learning. They are designed to monitor student progress in real-time and inform instructional decisions.

3. Which strategy is most effective for differentiating instruction in a diverse Special Education classroom?

A) Using the same teaching method for all students
B) Offering multiple means of representation, engagement, and expression
C) Providing identical assignments for every student
D) Focusing solely on the highest-achieving students

Answer: B) Offering multiple means of representation, engagement, and expression

Explanation: Differentiating instruction effectively involves offering multiple means of representation, engagement, and expression. This approach ensures that all students, regardless of their learning needs, have access to the curriculum in ways that suit their individual learning styles and preferences.

4. What is a primary benefit of involving students with special needs in self-assessment activities?

A) It reduces the need for teacher involvement
B) It helps students develop self-awareness and self-regulation skills
C) It minimizes the need for individualized instruction
D) It provides a way to compare students' performance to peers

Answer: B) It helps students develop self-awareness and self-regulation skills

Explanation: Involving students in self-assessment activities helps them develop self-awareness and self-regulation skills. This process encourages students to reflect on their own learning, set goals, and take ownership of their educational progress.

5. When designing an Individualized Education Program (IEP), which component is essential to include?

A) Generic academic goals
B) A description of the student's strengths and needs
C) A standard curriculum for all students
D) A focus only on behavioral issues

Answer: B) A description of the student's strengths and needs

Explanation: An essential component of an IEP is a description of the student's strengths and needs. This information helps in setting appropriate, individualized goals and planning the necessary supports and services to address the student's unique educational requirements.

6. What is the primary role of positive reinforcement in managing classroom behavior?

A) To punish students for undesirable behavior
B) To create a competitive environment among students
C) To encourage and reward desirable behavior
D) To minimize the need for clear expectations

Answer: C) To encourage and reward desirable behavior

Explanation: Positive reinforcement is used to encourage and reward desirable behavior. By providing incentives and praise for positive actions, educators can promote continued good behavior and motivate students to engage more effectively in the learning process.

7. Which type of data is most useful for evaluating the effectiveness of an instructional strategy?

A) National test scores
B) Teacher opinions
C) Student performance data and feedback
D) Parent surveys

Answer: C) Student performance data and feedback

Explanation: Student performance data and feedback are the most useful for evaluating the effectiveness of an instructional strategy. This data provides insights into how well the strategy is working and what adjustments may be needed to improve student outcomes.

8. In the context of Special Education, what is the purpose of an accommodation?

A) To change the content of the curriculum
B) To modify the way students access and demonstrate their learning
C) To alter the student's IEP goals
D) To remove the need for individualized support

Answer: B) To modify the way students access and demonstrate their learning

Explanation: Accommodations are intended to modify the way students access and demonstrate their learning without altering the content of the curriculum. They provide the necessary support to help students participate fully in educational activities.

9. What is a key factor to consider when selecting instructional materials for students with special needs?

A) The popularity of the materials among teachers
B) The materials' alignment with students' individual learning needs and goals
C) The cost of the materials
D) The ease of use for the teacher only

Answer: B) The materials' alignment with students' individual learning needs and goals

Explanation: When selecting instructional materials, it is crucial to ensure they align with students' individual learning needs and goals. This alignment helps to effectively address the specific requirements of each student and support their learning objectives.

10. Which strategy is most effective for fostering a positive classroom climate?

A) Establishing strict, inflexible rules
B) Encouraging open communication and mutual respect
C) Ignoring students' emotional needs
D) Focusing solely on academic achievement

Answer: B) Encouraging open communication and mutual respect

Explanation: Fostering a positive classroom climate is most effectively achieved by encouraging open communication and mutual respect. Creating an environment where students feel valued and heard promotes a supportive and collaborative learning atmosphere.

11. How can teachers effectively support students with behavioral challenges in the classroom?

A) By implementing a one-size-fits-all behavior management plan
B) By providing individualized behavior support plans based on specific needs
C) By ignoring behavioral issues and focusing only on academics
D) By using punitive measures to address all behavioral problems

Answer: B) By providing individualized behavior support plans based on specific needs

Explanation: Supporting students with behavioral challenges is best accomplished through individualized behavior support plans that address their specific needs. These plans provide targeted strategies and interventions to help manage and improve behavior.

12. Which of the following is an example of a formative assessment?

A) A state-mandated end-of-year test
B) A standardized achievement test
C) A weekly quiz or class activity
D) A mid-term exam

Answer: C) A weekly quiz or class activity

Explanation: A formative assessment, such as a weekly quiz or class activity, is used to monitor student progress and provide ongoing feedback. It helps educators make adjustments to instruction based on real-time data.

13. What is the purpose of using graphic organizers in instruction?

A) To reduce the need for visual aids
B) To provide a structured visual representation of information
C) To replace hands-on activities
D) To limit students' opportunities for creative expression

Answer: B) To provide a structured visual representation of information

Explanation: Graphic organizers are used to provide a structured visual representation of information, which helps students organize and understand content more effectively. They are particularly useful for students with special needs who may benefit from visual supports.

14. What is the best approach for integrating technology into instruction for students with special needs?

A) Using technology only as a reward
B) Selecting technology that aligns with students' individualized learning goals and needs
C) Using technology as a substitute for teacher interaction
D) Implementing technology without considering students' preferences

Answer: B) Selecting technology that aligns with students' individualized learning goals and needs

Explanation: Integrating technology into instruction should involve selecting tools that align with students' individualized learning goals and needs. This ensures that technology effectively supports and enhances their learning experiences.

15. What is the main benefit of involving students in setting their own learning goals?

A) It increases the teacher's workload
B) It promotes student ownership and motivation
C) It reduces the need for assessment
D) It makes grading more challenging

Answer: B) It promotes student ownership and motivation

Explanation: Involving students in setting their own learning goals promotes ownership and motivation by allowing them to take an active role in their educational progress. This approach encourages students to engage more deeply with their learning.

16. When planning an IEP meeting, what is a critical component to ensure its effectiveness?

A) Conducting the meeting without input from parents
B) Focusing solely on academic goals
C) Including all relevant stakeholders, such as parents, teachers, and specialists
D) Limiting discussion to the student's behavioral issues

Answer: C) Including all relevant stakeholders, such as parents, teachers, and specialists

Explanation: To ensure the effectiveness of an IEP meeting, it is critical to include all relevant stakeholders, including parents, teachers, and specialists. This collaborative approach ensures that all perspectives are considered in developing the IEP.

17. What is the role of peer-assisted learning in a Special Education classroom?

A) To create competition among students
B) To provide support and reinforcement through collaboration and interaction
C) To reduce the need for individualized instruction
D) To focus solely on academic achievement

Answer: B) To provide support and reinforcement through collaboration and interaction

Explanation: Peer-assisted learning provides support and reinforcement through collaboration and interaction. It enables students to work together, share knowledge, and support each other's learning, which can be particularly beneficial in a Special Education setting.

18. Which of the following strategies is most effective for teaching social skills to students with special needs?

A) Ignoring social skill development in favor of academic instruction
B) Using direct instruction and modeling of social skills
C) Focusing solely on academic goals
D) Allowing students to learn social skills solely through peer interactions

Answer: B) Using direct instruction and modeling of social skills

Explanation: Direct instruction and modeling of social skills are effective strategies for teaching social skills to students with special needs. These approaches provide clear examples and practice opportunities, helping students learn and apply appropriate social behaviors.

19. How can teachers effectively use data to inform their instruction?

A) By relying only on standardized test scores
B) By using a variety of assessment data to make informed instructional decisions
C) By ignoring data and focusing on intuition
D) By solely using student grades as a measure of success

Answer: B) By using a variety of assessment data to make informed instructional decisions

Explanation: Teachers can effectively use data to inform their instruction by utilizing a variety of assessment data. This approach provides a comprehensive view of student performance and helps in making informed decisions to improve teaching and learning.

20. What is a key consideration when creating an inclusive classroom environment for students with special needs?

A) Limiting interaction between students with and without disabilities
B) Ensuring that all students have equal access to learning opportunities and resources
C) Focusing only on physical accessibility
D) Using the same instructional materials for all students

Answer: B) Ensuring that all students have equal access to learning opportunities and resources

Explanation: Creating an inclusive classroom environment involves ensuring that all students have equal access to learning opportunities and resources. This includes adapting materials, activities, and teaching methods to meet the diverse needs of all students.

21. Which of the following is an effective way to monitor and assess student progress in a Special Education classroom?

A) Using periodic, high-stakes testing only
B) Relying solely on teacher observations
C) Implementing regular, varied assessments and tracking progress over time
D) Assessing students only at the end of each term

Answer: C) Implementing regular, varied assessments and tracking progress over time

Explanation: Effective monitoring and assessment of student progress involve implementing regular, varied assessments and tracking progress over time. This approach provides ongoing feedback and helps in making timely adjustments to instruction.

22. How can teachers best support students with sensory processing challenges in the classroom?

A) Ignoring sensory needs and focusing only on academic content
B) Providing sensory breaks and creating a sensory-friendly environment
C) Restricting access to sensory tools and supports
D) Using a one-size-fits-all approach for all students

Answer: B) Providing sensory breaks and creating a sensory-friendly environment

Explanation: To support students with sensory processing challenges, teachers should provide sensory breaks and create a sensory-friendly environment. This approach helps students manage sensory needs and improves their ability to focus and engage in learning activities.

23. What is the primary goal of implementing positive behavior support strategies in a Special Education setting?

A) To punish students for inappropriate behavior
B) To create a competitive classroom environment
C) To promote positive behavior and prevent challenging behaviors through proactive strategies
D) To focus only on academic instruction

Answer: C) To promote positive behavior and prevent challenging behaviors through proactive strategies

Explanation: The primary goal of implementing positive behavior support strategies is to promote positive behavior and prevent challenging behaviors through proactive, preventative strategies. This approach focuses on reinforcing desirable behavior and creating a supportive learning environment.

24. Which of the following practices is essential for effectively collaborating with other professionals in a Special Education setting?

A) Working independently without consulting others
B) Engaging in regular communication and sharing information
C) Limiting interactions to formal meetings only
D) Focusing solely on individual goals without considering team input

Answer: B) Engaging in regular communication and sharing information

Explanation: Effective collaboration with other professionals in a Special Education setting requires regular communication and sharing of information. This collaborative approach ensures that all team members are informed and working together to support student needs.

25. How can teachers use student data to differentiate instruction?

A) By using data to create a uniform teaching approach for all students
B) By analyzing data to identify individual learning needs and tailoring instruction accordingly
C) By focusing only on high-achieving students based on data
D) By using data to set rigid, one-size-fits-all goals

Answer: B) By analyzing data to identify individual learning needs and tailoring instruction accordingly

Explanation: Teachers can use student data to differentiate instruction by analyzing it to identify individual learning needs and tailoring instruction accordingly. This approach allows for targeted support that meets the specific requirements of each student.

26. What is the role of a transition plan in an IEP for students with special needs?

A) To provide a general outline of the student's academic goals
B) To prepare students for post-secondary education, employment, and independent living
C) To focus solely on classroom behavior management
D) To detail the teacher's responsibilities only

Answer: B) To prepare students for post-secondary education, employment, and independent living

Explanation: The role of a transition plan in an IEP is to prepare students for post-secondary education, employment, and independent living. This component of the IEP outlines the steps and supports needed to help students successfully transition from school to adult life.

27. What is an essential element of a well-structured lesson plan for students with special needs?

A) Ignoring students' prior knowledge
B) Clearly defined learning objectives and outcomes
C) Focusing only on lecture-based instruction
D) Using one teaching method for all students

Answer: B) Clearly defined learning objectives and outcomes

Explanation: An essential element of a well-structured lesson plan is clearly defined learning objectives and outcomes. This ensures that both the teacher and students understand the goals of the lesson and can measure progress effectively.

28. Which strategy is most effective for providing individualized support to students with autism in the classroom?

A) Implementing a one-size-fits-all behavioral management plan
B) Creating visual supports and schedules tailored to the student's needs
C) Ignoring sensory and communication needs
D) Relying solely on verbal instructions

Answer: B) Creating visual supports and schedules tailored to the student's needs

Explanation: For students with autism, creating visual supports and schedules tailored to their needs is most effective. Visual aids help these students understand expectations and routines, reducing anxiety and improving engagement.

29. What is the purpose of a behavioral intervention plan (BIP) in Special Education?

A) To eliminate academic goals
B) To address and modify challenging behaviors
C) To focus solely on physical accommodations
D) To change the curriculum content

Answer: B) To address and modify challenging behaviors

Explanation: A Behavioral Intervention Plan (BIP) is designed to address and modify challenging behaviors. It provides specific strategies and interventions to help manage and improve student behavior.

30. How can teachers effectively use student interests to enhance engagement in Special Education?

A) Ignoring students' interests and focusing only on the curriculum
B) Incorporating students' interests into lessons and activities
C) Providing the same activities for all students regardless of interest
D) Limiting activities to only academic content

Answer: B) Incorporating students' interests into lessons and activities

Explanation: Teachers can enhance engagement by incorporating students' interests into lessons and activities. This approach makes learning more relevant and motivating for students, increasing their participation and enthusiasm.

31. Which of the following is a key consideration when using assistive technology in the classroom?

A) Using technology that is the most expensive
B) Selecting technology that aligns with the student's specific needs and goals
C) Relying solely on technology for instruction
D) Implementing technology without student input

Answer: B) Selecting technology that aligns with the student's specific needs and goals

Explanation: When using assistive technology, it is crucial to select tools that align with the student's specific needs and goals. This ensures that the technology effectively supports and enhances their learning experience.

32. What role does data analysis play in differentiating instruction for students with special needs?

A) It provides a way to rank students based on performance
B) It helps educators tailor instruction to meet individual learning needs
C) It determines the overall classroom behavior
D) It is used solely for administrative purposes

Answer: B) It helps educators tailor instruction to meet individual learning needs

Explanation: Data analysis helps educators tailor instruction to meet individual learning needs by providing insights into students' strengths, weaknesses, and progress. This information is used to adjust teaching strategies and supports effectively.

33. How can teachers promote a growth mindset among students with special needs?

A) Focusing only on students' academic performance
B) Encouraging students to view challenges as opportunities for growth and learning
C) Avoiding feedback on areas of struggle
D) Maintaining a fixed approach to instruction

Answer: B) Encouraging students to view challenges as opportunities for growth and learning

Explanation: Promoting a growth mindset involves encouraging students to view challenges as opportunities for growth and learning. This mindset helps students develop resilience and a positive attitude towards their efforts and achievements.

34. What is an appropriate method for assessing the effectiveness of instructional accommodations?

A) Relying solely on end-of-year tests
B) Observing and evaluating student progress and response to accommodations
C) Using only teacher's subjective opinions
D) Comparing students' scores to a national average

Answer: B) Observing and evaluating student progress and response to accommodations

Explanation: To assess the effectiveness of instructional accommodations, it is important to observe and evaluate student progress and their response to the accommodations. This approach provides direct feedback on how well the supports are working.

35. Which strategy best supports students with executive functioning challenges in the classroom?

A) Providing complex, unstructured tasks
B) Offering clear, step-by-step instructions and routines
C) Ignoring organizational needs and focusing only on content
D) Allowing students to work without any structure

Answer: B) Offering clear, step-by-step instructions and routines

Explanation: For students with executive functioning challenges, offering clear, step-by-step instructions and routines is the most effective strategy. This helps them organize their tasks, manage time, and follow through with assignments.

36. What is the primary goal of using social stories with students with special needs?

A) To focus only on academic content
B) To help students understand and navigate social situations
C) To replace individualized instruction
D) To limit interaction with peers

Answer: B) To help students understand and navigate social situations

Explanation: Social stories are used to help students understand and navigate social situations by providing clear, descriptive, and often visual explanations of social norms and expectations. This tool is particularly beneficial for students with social and communication challenges.

37. How should teachers approach the assessment of students with diverse learning needs?

A) Using the same assessment tools for all students
B) Employing a variety of assessment methods to accommodate diverse needs
C) Ignoring individual learning needs in assessments

D) Focusing only on standardized testing

Answer: B) Employing a variety of assessment methods to accommodate diverse needs

Explanation: Teachers should use a variety of assessment methods to accommodate diverse learning needs. This approach ensures that all students have multiple opportunities to demonstrate their understanding and skills in ways that suit their abilities.

38. What is a key benefit of collaborative teaching models in Special Education?

A) Reducing the need for individualized support
B) Allowing teachers to work together to address diverse student needs and provide targeted support
C) Limiting the amount of planning required
D) Creating a competitive classroom environment

Answer: B) Allowing teachers to work together to address diverse student needs and provide targeted support

Explanation: Collaborative teaching models benefit from allowing teachers to work together to address diverse student needs and provide targeted support. This teamwork enhances instructional practices and ensures that all students receive the necessary support.

39. What is an effective way to involve students with special needs in setting their own learning goals?

A) Setting goals for students without their input
B) Engaging students in discussions about their strengths, interests, and areas for improvement to set personalized goals
C) Providing generic goals for all students
D) Limiting goal-setting to academic content only

Answer: B) Engaging students in discussions about their strengths, interests, and areas for improvement to set personalized goals

Explanation: An effective way to involve students in setting their own learning goals is to engage them in discussions about their strengths, interests, and areas for improvement. This approach helps students set personalized and meaningful goals that are relevant to their individual needs.

40. Which strategy is most effective for supporting students with dyslexia in the classroom?

A) Ignoring reading difficulties and focusing only on other subjects
B) Providing specialized reading instruction and using multisensory learning approaches
C) Restricting access to reading materials
D) Using only traditional reading methods

Answer: B) Providing specialized reading instruction and using multisensory learning approaches

Explanation: For students with dyslexia, providing specialized reading instruction and using multisensory learning approaches are most effective. These strategies help students develop reading skills through multiple sensory channels and personalized support.

41. How can teachers support the transition from elementary to middle school for students with special needs?

A) Ignoring the transition process and focusing only on academic content
B) Providing a structured transition plan that includes orientation, support, and gradual adjustment
C) Relying solely on student self-adjustment
D) Limiting communication with middle school staff

Answer: B) Providing a structured transition plan that includes orientation, support, and gradual adjustment

Explanation: Supporting the transition from elementary to middle school involves providing a structured transition plan that includes orientation, support, and gradual adjustment. This helps students adapt to new environments and expectations effectively.

42. What is a key consideration when developing a student's individualized instruction plan?

A) Focusing only on academic standards without considering student needs
B) Incorporating specific, measurable goals based on the student's unique learning needs and strengths
C) Using a generic plan for all students
D) Ignoring feedback from the student and their family

Answer: B) Incorporating specific, measurable goals based on the student's unique learning needs and strengths

Explanation: When developing an individualized instruction plan, it is essential to incorporate specific, measurable goals based on the student's unique learning needs and strengths. This approach ensures that the plan is tailored to support the student's individual progress.

43. What role do accommodations play in supporting students with physical disabilities in the classroom?

A) Changing the content of the curriculum
B) Modifying how students access and participate in learning activities
C) Eliminating the need for individualized instruction
D) Ignoring physical accessibility needs

Answer: B) Modifying how students access and participate in learning activities

Explanation: Accommodations support students with physical disabilities by modifying how they access and participate in learning activities. This includes providing physical adjustments and supports to ensure that students can engage effectively in the classroom.

44. Which practice is effective for promoting self-advocacy skills in students with special needs?

A) Making all decisions for the students without their input
B) Encouraging students to participate in IEP meetings and express their own needs and preferences
C) Ignoring students' opinions and focusing solely on academic goals
D) Limiting students' involvement in decision-making processes

Answer: B) Encouraging students to participate in IEP meetings and express their own needs and preferences

Explanation: Promoting self-advocacy skills involves encouraging students to participate in IEP meetings and express their own needs and preferences. This practice helps students develop the skills to advocate for themselves and take an active role in their education.

45. What is an important consideration when adapting classroom materials for students with visual impairments?

A) Using only standard print materials
B) Providing materials in accessible formats, such as large print or braille
C) Ignoring the need for material adaptation
D) Limiting access to specialized materials

Answer: B) Providing materials in accessible formats, such as large print or braille

Explanation: When adapting classroom materials for students with visual impairments, it is important to provide materials in accessible formats, such as large print or braille. This ensures that students can access and engage with the learning content effectively.

46. How can teachers use peer-assisted learning effectively in a Special Education setting?

A) Assigning students to work in isolation
B) Encouraging students to work together on tasks and support each other's learning
C) Limiting peer interactions to avoid distractions
D) Using only teacher-led instruction

Answer: B) Encouraging students to work together on tasks and support each other's learning

Explanation: Peer-assisted learning is effective when students work together on tasks and support each other's learning. This approach fosters collaboration, builds social skills, and provides additional support for students who may benefit from peer interactions.

47. What is the purpose of a transition plan in an IEP for older students?

A) To detail academic content only
B) To prepare students for life after school, including employment, education, and independent living
C) To focus solely on classroom behavior
D) To outline daily classroom routines

Answer: B) To prepare students for life after school, including employment, education, and independent living

Explanation: The purpose of a transition plan in an IEP for older students is to prepare them for life after school, including employment, education, and independent living. This plan outlines the steps and supports needed to help students transition successfully to adulthood.

48. What is an effective strategy for supporting students with ADHD in managing classroom tasks?

A) Providing unstructured, open-ended tasks
B) Using clear, organized routines and visual reminders
C) Ignoring the need for task management support
D) Allowing students to work without any guidelines

Answer: B) Using clear, organized routines and visual reminders

Explanation: To support students with ADHD in managing classroom tasks, using clear, organized routines and visual reminders is effective. These strategies help students stay focused and organized, making it easier for them to complete tasks and follow instructions.

49. How can teachers ensure that their instruction is culturally responsive for students with special needs?

A) Using a standardized approach for all students
B) Incorporating students' cultural backgrounds and experiences into the curriculum and instruction
C) Ignoring cultural differences and focusing only on academic content
D) Using only culturally specific materials for all students

Answer: B) Incorporating students' cultural backgrounds and experiences into the curriculum and instruction

Explanation: To ensure culturally responsive instruction, teachers should incorporate students' cultural backgrounds and experiences into the curriculum and instruction. This approach respects and values diversity, making learning more relevant and inclusive for all students.

50. What is the role of a special education teacher in a co-teaching model?

A) To work independently from the general education teacher
B) To collaborate with the general education teacher to plan and deliver instruction for all students
C) To focus only on students with special needs without involving the general education teacher
D) To limit involvement in classroom activities

Answer: B) To collaborate with the general education teacher to plan and deliver instruction for all students

Explanation: In a co-teaching model, the special education teacher collaborates with the general education teacher to plan and deliver instruction for all students. This collaborative approach ensures that the needs of all students are met through shared expertise and resources.

51. What is a key consideration when setting up a behavior management system for students with special needs?

A) Using a one-size-fits-all approach
B) Tailoring the system to individual student needs and behaviors
C) Focusing only on punitive measures
D) Ignoring input from students and their families

Answer: B) Tailoring the system to individual student needs and behaviors

Explanation: When setting up a behavior management system, it is crucial to tailor the system to individual student needs and behaviors. This personalized approach ensures that the strategies used are effective and appropriate for each student's specific situation.

52. How can teachers use formative assessment to support students with special needs?

A) By providing feedback only at the end of the term
B) By using regular, ongoing assessments to monitor progress and adjust instruction
C) By focusing solely on summative assessments
D) By assessing students only once during the school year

Answer: B) By using regular, ongoing assessments to monitor progress and adjust instruction

Explanation: Formative assessment supports students with special needs by providing regular, ongoing feedback that helps monitor progress and adjust instruction. This approach allows for timely interventions and adjustments based on students' needs.

53. What is the benefit of using flexible grouping in a Special Education classroom?

A) Creating fixed, unchangeable groups
B) Allowing students to work in different group configurations based on their needs and the task
C) Limiting students' interaction with peers
D) Maintaining a rigid group structure throughout the year

Answer: B) Allowing students to work in different group configurations based on their needs and the task

Explanation: Flexible grouping allows students to work in different group configurations based on their needs and the task at hand. This approach provides varied social and learning opportunities, accommodating diverse learning styles and abilities.

54. How can teachers effectively use self-assessment with students with special needs?

A) Ignoring students' self-assessment and focusing only on teacher assessments
B) Encouraging students to reflect on their own learning and set personal goals
C) Using self-assessment as the sole measure of student progress
D) Limiting opportunities for self-assessment

Answer: B) Encouraging students to reflect on their own learning and set personal goals

Explanation: Effective use of self-assessment involves encouraging students to reflect on their own learning and set personal goals. This practice helps students develop self-awareness and take ownership of their learning process.

55. What is a key principle of Universal Design for Learning (UDL) in Special Education?

A) Using a single teaching method for all students
B) Providing multiple means of representation, engagement, and action/expression to accommodate diverse learners
C) Focusing solely on academic content
D) Limiting instructional strategies to a specific approach

Answer: B) Providing multiple means of representation, engagement, and action/expression to accommodate diverse learners

Explanation: Universal Design for Learning (UDL) is based on the principle of providing multiple means of representation, engagement, and action/expression to accommodate diverse learners. This approach ensures that all students have equal access to learning opportunities.

56. What is the role of student self-monitoring in a Special Education setting?

A) To rely solely on teacher monitoring
B) To help students track their own progress and develop independence
C) To eliminate the need for teacher feedback
D) To focus only on academic performance without considering behavior

Answer: B) To help students track their own progress and develop independence

Explanation: Student self-monitoring helps students track their own progress and develop independence. This practice encourages self-regulation and responsibility for their learning and behavior.

57. How can teachers support students with special needs in developing effective study habits?

A) Providing unstructured study time without guidance
B) Teaching specific study skills and strategies, and providing practice opportunities
C) Ignoring the need for study skills instruction
D) Relying solely on memorization techniques

Answer: B) Teaching specific study skills and strategies, and providing practice opportunities

Explanation: To support students with special needs in developing effective study habits, teachers should teach specific study skills and strategies and provide practice opportunities. This approach helps students build effective habits for academic success.

58. What is an effective way to involve families in the Special Education process?

A) Limiting communication to formal meetings only
B) Engaging families in ongoing communication and collaboration regarding their child's needs and progress
C) Ignoring family input in decision-making processes
D) Providing information only in written form without opportunities for discussion

Answer: B) Engaging families in ongoing communication and collaboration regarding their child's needs and progress

Explanation: Involving families in the Special Education process is effective when there is ongoing communication and collaboration regarding their child's needs and progress. This partnership ensures that families are informed and can contribute valuable insights and support.

59. How can teachers use visual supports to enhance learning for students with special needs?

A) Using visual aids only for decorative purposes
B) Providing visual schedules, charts, and cues to support understanding and organization

C) Limiting the use of visual supports to specific subjects
D) Avoiding visual supports in favor of verbal instructions

Answer: B) Providing visual schedules, charts, and cues to support understanding and organization

Explanation: Visual supports, such as schedules, charts, and cues, enhance learning for students with special needs by supporting understanding and organization. These tools help students follow routines, understand expectations, and stay engaged.

60. What is a critical factor in developing effective goals in an IEP?

A) Setting vague, non-specific goals
B) Developing SMART (Specific, Measurable, Achievable, Relevant, Time-bound) goals that address the student's unique needs
C) Creating goals that are not aligned with the student's strengths and weaknesses
D) Using generic goals that apply to all students

Answer: B) Developing SMART (Specific, Measurable, Achievable, Relevant, Time-bound) goals that address the student's unique needs

Explanation: Developing SMART goals in an IEP ensures that goals are specific, measurable, achievable, relevant, and time-bound. This approach addresses the student's unique needs and provides clear criteria for measuring progress.

61. How can teachers effectively support students with sensory processing disorders in the classroom?

A) Ignoring sensory needs and focusing only on academic instruction
B) Creating a sensory-friendly environment and providing sensory breaks as needed
C) Restricting access to sensory tools and accommodations
D) Providing only verbal instructions without considering sensory needs

Answer: B) Creating a sensory-friendly environment and providing sensory breaks as needed

Explanation: To support students with sensory processing disorders, teachers should create a sensory-friendly environment and provide sensory breaks as needed. These accommodations help students manage sensory sensitivities and maintain focus in the classroom.

62. What is an effective approach to modifying assignments for students with special needs?

A) Using the same assignments for all students without modifications
B) Adapting assignments to match the student's level of understanding and provide appropriate challenges
C) Ignoring individual differences in assignment modifications

D) Providing assignments that are unrelated to the curriculum

Answer: B) Adapting assignments to match the student's level of understanding and provide appropriate challenges

Explanation: Modifying assignments effectively involves adapting them to match the student's level of understanding and providing appropriate challenges. This approach ensures that assignments are accessible and meaningful for each student.

63. What is the purpose of conducting a functional behavior assessment (FBA) in Special Education?

A) To identify academic strengths and weaknesses
B) To understand the reasons behind challenging behaviors and develop effective interventions
C) To determine the student's eligibility for special education services
D) To create a fixed behavior management plan without adjustments

Answer: B) To understand the reasons behind challenging behaviors and develop effective interventions

Explanation: The purpose of conducting a Functional Behavior Assessment (FBA) is to understand the reasons behind challenging behaviors and develop effective interventions. This assessment helps identify the triggers and functions of behaviors, guiding the creation of targeted behavior support plans.

64. How can teachers support students with special needs in developing social skills?

A) Focusing only on academic content and ignoring social skill development
B) Providing structured opportunities for social interaction and teaching specific social skills
C) Limiting social interactions to avoid distractions
D) Using only informal methods to teach social skills

Answer: B) Providing structured opportunities for social interaction and teaching specific social skills

Explanation: Supporting students with special needs in developing social skills involves providing structured opportunities for social interaction and teaching specific social skills. This approach helps students practice and improve their social abilities in a supportive environment.

65. What is an important consideration when designing a classroom environment for students with physical disabilities?

A) Using standard classroom furniture and layout
B) Ensuring that the classroom is accessible and accommodates mobility needs, such as ramps and adapted seating
C) Ignoring physical accessibility requirements

D) Limiting access to classroom resources

Answer: B) Ensuring that the classroom is accessible and accommodates mobility needs, such as ramps and adapted seating

Explanation: When designing a classroom environment for students with physical disabilities, it is important to ensure accessibility and accommodate mobility needs. This includes providing ramps, adapted seating, and other modifications to ensure that all students can navigate and participate in the classroom.

66. How can teachers effectively use technology to support students with special needs?

A) Relying only on traditional teaching methods without incorporating technology
B) Integrating technology tools that align with the student's learning goals and needs
C) Using technology without considering the student's individual needs
D) Limiting technology use to specific subjects

Answer: B) Integrating technology tools that align with the student's learning goals and needs

Explanation: Effectively using technology to support students with special needs involves integrating technology tools that align with the student's learning goals and needs. This approach ensures that technology enhances learning and provides meaningful support.

67. What is the role of peer support in a Special Education classroom?

A) To create a competitive environment among students
B) To provide additional academic and social support through peer interactions
C) To limit peer interactions and focus only on individual work
D) To replace the need for teacher support

Answer: B) To provide additional academic and social support through peer interactions

Explanation: Peer support in a Special Education classroom provides additional academic and social support through peer interactions. This approach helps students learn from and assist each other, fostering a collaborative and inclusive learning environment.

68. How can teachers use positive reinforcement effectively in managing classroom behavior?

A) Ignoring positive behaviors and focusing only on misbehavior
B) Providing specific, immediate rewards or praise for desired behaviors to encourage repetition
C) Using punishment as the primary method for behavior management
D) Offering rewards only for academic achievements

Answer: B) Providing specific, immediate rewards or praise for desired behaviors to encourage repetition

Explanation: Positive reinforcement is effective when teachers provide specific, immediate rewards or praise for desired behaviors. This approach encourages students to repeat positive behaviors and helps build a positive classroom environment.

69. What is an effective way to support students with communication disorders in the classroom?

A) Using only verbal instructions without additional supports
B) Providing alternative communication methods, such as picture boards or speech-generating devices
C) Ignoring communication needs and focusing solely on academic content
D) Limiting communication to written form only

Answer: B) Providing alternative communication methods, such as picture boards or speech-generating devices

Explanation: Supporting students with communication disorders involves providing alternative communication methods, such as picture boards or speech-generating devices. These tools help students express themselves and participate in classroom activities effectively.

70. How can teachers create an inclusive classroom environment for students with diverse learning needs?

A) Using a one-size-fits-all approach to instruction
B) Implementing practices that accommodate and celebrate diversity, including varied teaching methods and materials
C) Ignoring differences among students and focusing on a single teaching method
D) Restricting participation based on ability levels

Answer: B) Implementing practices that accommodate and celebrate diversity, including varied teaching methods and materials

Explanation: Creating an inclusive classroom environment involves implementing practices that accommodate and celebrate diversity. This includes using varied teaching methods and materials to address different learning needs and ensuring all students feel valued and supported.

71. What is the importance of collaboration between special education teachers and general education teachers?

A) To separate instruction for students with special needs from the general classroom instruction
B) To share expertise and strategies to better support all students in the classroom
C) To limit communication and coordination between teachers

D) To focus solely on individual teacher responsibilities

Answer: B) To share expertise and strategies to better support all students in the classroom

Explanation: Collaboration between special education teachers and general education teachers is important for sharing expertise and strategies to better support all students in the classroom. This teamwork enhances instruction and ensures that the diverse needs of students are met.

72. How can teachers use formative feedback to improve student learning outcomes?

A) Providing feedback only at the end of a unit or term
B) Offering regular, specific feedback throughout the learning process to guide improvement
C) Focusing only on final assessments without ongoing feedback
D) Ignoring feedback and relying solely on student self-assessment

Answer: B) Offering regular, specific feedback throughout the learning process to guide improvement

Explanation: Formative feedback is most effective when it is regular and specific, guiding students throughout the learning process. This type of feedback helps students understand their progress and make necessary adjustments to improve their learning outcomes.

73. What is a critical factor in designing effective classroom accommodations for students with special needs?

A) Using the same accommodations for all students regardless of their individual needs
B) Tailoring accommodations to address specific challenges and needs of each student
C) Limiting accommodations to only physical adjustments
D) Ignoring input from students and their families

Answer: B) Tailoring accommodations to address specific challenges and needs of each student

Explanation: Designing effective classroom accommodations requires tailoring them to address the specific challenges and needs of each student. Personalized accommodations ensure that students receive the appropriate support to access and participate in learning activities.

74. How can teachers support students with emotional and behavioral disorders in managing classroom behavior?

A) Using punitive measures exclusively
B) Implementing positive behavior interventions and supports (PBIS) and providing consistent, supportive responses
C) Ignoring behavioral issues and focusing only on academic instruction
D) Limiting opportunities for social interaction

Answer: B) Implementing positive behavior interventions and supports (PBIS) and providing consistent, supportive responses

Explanation: Supporting students with emotional and behavioral disorders involves implementing positive behavior interventions and supports (PBIS) and providing consistent, supportive responses. This approach helps manage behavior effectively and creates a positive learning environment.

75. What is the role of an Individualized Education Program (IEP) in Special Education?

A) To provide a generic curriculum for all students
B) To outline personalized goals, accommodations, and supports based on the student's unique needs
C) To limit the scope of instruction to basic skills only
D) To create a fixed educational plan without room for adjustments

Answer: B) To outline personalized goals, accommodations, and supports based on the student's unique needs

Explanation: The role of an Individualized Education Program (IEP) is to outline personalized goals, accommodations, and supports based on the student's unique needs. This individualized plan ensures that the educational requirements of each student with special needs are addressed effectively.

76. How can teachers support students with learning disabilities in developing reading skills?

A) Using only traditional reading instruction methods
B) Implementing evidence-based strategies such as phonics instruction and reading interventions tailored to the student's needs
C) Ignoring the need for specialized reading instruction
D) Limiting reading activities to simple texts only

Answer: B) Implementing evidence-based strategies such as phonics instruction and reading interventions tailored to the student's needs

Explanation: Supporting students with learning disabilities in developing reading skills involves implementing evidence-based strategies, such as phonics instruction and targeted reading interventions. These approaches are tailored to meet the specific needs of students and enhance their reading abilities.

77. What is an important consideration when implementing assistive technology in a Special Education classroom?

A) Using technology that is not user-friendly or accessible
B) Ensuring that assistive technology is appropriate for the student's needs and provides meaningful support

C) Limiting technology use to specific subjects
D) Ignoring student preferences and needs in technology selection

Answer: B) Ensuring that assistive technology is appropriate for the student's needs and provides meaningful support

Explanation: When implementing assistive technology in a Special Education classroom, it is important to ensure that the technology is appropriate for the student's needs and provides meaningful support. This consideration ensures that the technology effectively enhances the student's learning experience.

78. How can teachers effectively address the needs of students with Autism Spectrum Disorder (ASD) in the classroom?

A) Using a one-size-fits-all approach to instruction
B) Implementing structured routines, visual supports, and individualized interventions tailored to the student's needs
C) Ignoring the need for individualized supports and focusing solely on academic content
D) Limiting interactions and social opportunities

Answer: B) Implementing structured routines, visual supports, and individualized interventions tailored to the student's needs

Explanation: To address the needs of students with Autism Spectrum Disorder (ASD), teachers should implement structured routines, visual supports, and individualized interventions tailored to the student's needs. These strategies help create a supportive and predictable learning environment.

79. What is the role of collaboration with specialists in supporting students with special needs?

A) To replace classroom instruction with specialist-led sessions
B) To provide additional expertise and resources that enhance support for students with special needs
C) To limit the involvement of specialists in the classroom
D) To focus solely on academic instruction without considering specialist input

Answer: B) To provide additional expertise and resources that enhance support for students with special needs

Explanation: Collaboration with specialists provides additional expertise and resources that enhance support for students with special needs. Specialists can offer valuable insights, strategies, and interventions that complement classroom instruction and address specific needs.

80. How can teachers ensure that assessment practices are fair and equitable for students with special needs?

A) Using the same assessment methods for all students without modifications
B) Implementing accommodations and modifications to ensure assessments are accessible and reflect students' true abilities
C) Ignoring individual needs in assessment practices
D) Focusing only on summative assessments without considering formative assessments

Answer: B) Implementing accommodations and modifications to ensure assessments are accessible and reflect students' true abilities

Explanation: To ensure that assessment practices are fair and equitable for students with special needs, it is essential to implement accommodations and modifications. These adjustments help ensure that assessments are accessible and accurately reflect students' abilities, providing a fair evaluation of their knowledge and skills.

81. What is the primary goal of differentiated instruction in a Special Education classroom?

A) To provide the same instruction to all students
B) To tailor instruction to meet the diverse needs of each student
C) To limit instruction to a single teaching method
D) To focus solely on group work without individual attention

Answer: B) To tailor instruction to meet the diverse needs of each student

Explanation: Differentiated instruction aims to tailor teaching methods and materials to meet the diverse needs of each student, ensuring that all learners have access to appropriate challenges and supports.

82. How can teachers support students with dyslexia in improving their writing skills?

A) Using only traditional writing assignments
B) Providing assistive technology, such as word processors with spell check and dictation software
C) Ignoring the need for writing supports
D) Focusing solely on handwriting practice

Answer: B) Providing assistive technology, such as word processors with spell check and dictation software

Explanation: To support students with dyslexia in improving their writing skills, providing assistive technology like word processors with spell check and dictation software can be very effective. These tools help manage spelling and writing difficulties.

83. What is an effective strategy for managing transitions for students with Autism Spectrum Disorder (ASD)?

A) Making transitions abrupt and unstructured
B) Providing advance notice, visual schedules, and clear cues for transitions
C) Ignoring the need for transition supports
D) Allowing students to transition at their own pace without guidance

Answer: B) Providing advance notice, visual schedules, and clear cues for transitions

Explanation: Effective strategies for managing transitions for students with ASD include providing advance notice, visual schedules, and clear cues. These supports help students prepare for and adapt to changes in routines or activities.

84. How can teachers use scaffolding to support students with special needs?

A) Providing no support and expecting students to figure things out independently
B) Offering temporary, structured support that gradually decreases as students gain competence
C) Using a one-size-fits-all approach to instruction
D) Focusing solely on independent work without guidance

Answer: B) Offering temporary, structured support that gradually decreases as students gain competence

Explanation: Scaffolding involves offering temporary, structured support to students that gradually decreases as they gain competence. This approach helps students build skills and confidence progressively.

85. What is the purpose of using graphic organizers in a Special Education classroom?

A) To limit visual aids to specific subjects
B) To help students organize and understand information visually
C) To focus only on verbal instructions
D) To avoid using any visual supports

Answer: B) To help students organize and understand information visually

Explanation: Graphic organizers are used to help students visually organize and understand information. They provide a structured way for students to process and make connections between concepts.

86. How can teachers effectively use positive behavior supports in a Special Education setting?

A) By using punishment as the primary behavior management strategy
B) By implementing a system of rewards and positive reinforcement to encourage desirable behaviors
C) By focusing solely on academic instruction without considering behavior
D) By ignoring behavioral issues and focusing on individual work

Answer: B) By implementing a system of rewards and positive reinforcement to encourage desirable behaviors

Explanation: Positive behavior supports involve using a system of rewards and positive reinforcement to encourage desirable behaviors. This approach helps create a supportive and motivating classroom environment.

87. What is the role of a behavior intervention plan (BIP) in supporting students with challenging behaviors?

A) To ignore challenging behaviors and focus on academic content
B) To outline specific strategies and supports to address and manage challenging behaviors
C) To provide a generic behavior management plan for all students
D) To focus solely on punishing misbehavior

Answer: B) To outline specific strategies and supports to address and manage challenging behaviors

Explanation: A behavior intervention plan (BIP) outlines specific strategies and supports to address and manage challenging behaviors. It provides a structured approach to behavior management tailored to individual student needs.

88. How can teachers use visual schedules to support students with special needs?

A) Providing schedules only in verbal form
B) Using visual schedules to help students understand and anticipate daily routines and transitions
C) Ignoring the need for visual supports in favor of verbal instructions
D) Using visual schedules only for specific subjects

Answer: B) Using visual schedules to help students understand and anticipate daily routines and transitions

Explanation: Visual schedules help students with special needs understand and anticipate daily routines and transitions. They provide a clear and visual representation of what to expect throughout the day.

89. What is an important consideration when setting up a sensory-friendly classroom environment?

A) Ignoring sensory needs and using standard classroom arrangements
B) Creating a space with sensory tools and calming activities to support sensory regulation
C) Limiting sensory tools and focusing solely on academic instruction
D) Using only verbal instructions without considering sensory needs

Answer: B) Creating a space with sensory tools and calming activities to support sensory regulation

Explanation: An important consideration for a sensory-friendly classroom environment is creating a space with sensory tools and calming activities. This supports sensory regulation and helps students manage sensory sensitivities.

90. How can teachers use differentiated assessments to support students with special needs?

A) Using a single assessment method for all students
B) Implementing various assessment methods tailored to different learning styles and needs
C) Ignoring individual differences in assessment practices
D) Focusing only on summative assessments

Answer: B) Implementing various assessment methods tailored to different learning styles and needs

Explanation: Differentiated assessments involve using various methods tailored to different learning styles and needs. This approach ensures that assessments accurately reflect each student's understanding and abilities.

91. What is the benefit of involving students in setting their own learning goals?

A) Limiting student involvement in their learning process
B) Encouraging students to take ownership of their learning and set personal goals
C) Ignoring student input and focusing solely on teacher-set goals
D) Creating fixed goals without considering student preferences

Answer: B) Encouraging students to take ownership of their learning and set personal goals

Explanation: Involving students in setting their own learning goals encourages them to take ownership of their learning and fosters motivation and self-regulation. This practice helps students become more engaged and invested in their education.

92. How can teachers effectively support students with anxiety in the classroom?

A) Ignoring anxiety-related concerns and focusing solely on academic content
B) Providing a supportive environment with strategies to manage anxiety, such as relaxation techniques and predictable routines
C) Limiting support to individual work only
D) Using punitive measures to address anxiety-related behaviors

Answer: B) Providing a supportive environment with strategies to manage anxiety, such as relaxation techniques and predictable routines

Explanation: Supporting students with anxiety involves providing a supportive environment with strategies to manage anxiety, such as relaxation techniques and predictable routines. This approach helps reduce anxiety and promotes a positive learning experience.

93. What is the role of peer tutoring in supporting students with special needs?

A) To provide a competitive learning environment
B) To offer additional support and reinforcement through peer interactions
C) To limit peer interactions and focus only on teacher-led instruction
D) To replace individualized instruction with peer-led sessions

Answer: B) To offer additional support and reinforcement through peer interactions

Explanation: Peer tutoring provides additional support and reinforcement through peer interactions. This approach allows students to benefit from collaborative learning and receive assistance from their classmates.

94. How can teachers use self-regulation strategies to support students with special needs?

A) Ignoring the need for self-regulation and focusing solely on external controls
B) Teaching students strategies to manage their own emotions and behaviors, such as mindfulness and self-monitoring
C) Providing no support for self-regulation and relying only on teacher management
D) Limiting opportunities for self-regulation practice

Answer: B) Teaching students strategies to manage their own emotions and behaviors, such as mindfulness and self-monitoring

Explanation: Supporting students with special needs in developing self-regulation involves teaching strategies to manage their own emotions and behaviors, such as mindfulness and self-monitoring. These strategies help students become more independent and effective in managing their own behavior.

95. What is a key principle of using Universal Design for Learning (UDL) in Special Education?

A) Providing a single method of instruction for all students
B) Offering multiple means of engagement, representation, and action/expression to accommodate diverse learners
C) Limiting instructional methods to traditional approaches
D) Focusing only on academic content without considering learner variability

Answer: B) Offering multiple means of engagement, representation, and action/expression to accommodate diverse learners

Explanation: Universal Design for Learning (UDL) involves offering multiple means of engagement, representation, and action/expression to accommodate diverse learners. This approach ensures that all students have access to learning opportunities in ways that suit their individual needs.

96. How can teachers effectively use accommodations to support students with special needs during assessments?

A) Using the same assessment for all students without modifications
B) Implementing accommodations such as extended time, alternate formats, or assistive technology to ensure equitable access
C) Ignoring the need for accommodations and focusing solely on standard assessments
D) Providing accommodations only for specific types of assessments

Answer: B) Implementing accommodations such as extended time, alternate formats, or assistive technology to ensure equitable access

Explanation: Effective use of accommodations during assessments involves implementing modifications such as extended time, alternate formats, or assistive technology. These accommodations ensure that students with special needs have equitable access to demonstrating their knowledge and skills.

97. What is an important factor in building positive relationships with students with special needs?

A) Focusing only on academic performance without considering personal connections
B) Developing trust and open communication, and showing empathy and understanding
C) Limiting interactions to formal settings only
D) Ignoring individual differences and focusing solely on group dynamics

Answer: B) Developing trust and open communication, and showing empathy and understanding

Explanation: Building positive relationships with students with special needs involves developing trust and open communication, and showing empathy and understanding. These factors contribute to a supportive and respectful learning environment.

98. How can teachers effectively use formative assessments to inform instruction for students with special needs?

A) Providing feedback only after summative assessments
B) Using formative assessments to gather ongoing information about student progress and adjust instruction accordingly
C) Focusing solely on summative assessments for evaluation
D) Ignoring formative assessments in favor of end-of-term evaluations

Answer: B) Using formative assessments to gather ongoing information about student progress and adjust instruction accordingly

Explanation: Formative assessments are used to gather ongoing information about student progress and adjust instruction as needed. This approach helps teachers identify areas where students may need additional support and make timely instructional adjustments.

99. What is a key consideration when developing individualized learning materials for students with special needs?

A) Using the same materials for all students regardless of their needs
B) Tailoring materials to address the specific learning needs and preferences of each student
C) Limiting the use of individualized materials in favor of standard resources
D) Ignoring student preferences and using only generic materials

Answer: B) Tailoring materials to address the specific learning needs and preferences of each student

Explanation: Developing individualized learning materials involves tailoring them to address the specific learning needs and preferences of each student. This approach ensures that materials are effective and engaging for each learner.

100. How can teachers support students with executive function challenges in organizing their work?

A) Providing no organizational supports and expecting students to manage independently
B) Offering tools and strategies such as planners, checklists, and organizational aids to help students manage their tasks
C) Ignoring executive function challenges and focusing only on academic content
D) Limiting organizational supports to specific subjects

Answer: B) Offering tools and strategies such as planners, checklists, and organizational aids to help students manage their tasks

Explanation: Supporting students with executive function challenges involves offering tools and strategies like planners, checklists, and organizational aids. These supports help students manage their tasks and stay organized.

101. What is an important strategy for involving families in the educational process of students with special needs?

A) Limiting communication with families to formal meetings only
B) Encouraging regular, open communication and collaboration between teachers and families to support the student's needs
C) Ignoring family input and focusing solely on classroom instruction
D) Providing only written updates without opportunities for discussion

Answer: B) Encouraging regular, open communication and collaboration between teachers and families to support the student's needs

Explanation: Involving families in the educational process is best achieved through regular, open communication and collaboration. This partnership helps ensure that families are informed and can contribute to supporting their child's learning and development.

102. How can teachers use behavior contracts to support students with behavioral challenges?

A) Creating a fixed contract without input from the student
B) Developing a collaborative behavior contract with clear expectations, rewards, and consequences that involve the student
C) Ignoring the need for behavior contracts and using only general classroom rules
D) Limiting behavior contracts to academic behavior only

Answer: B) Developing a collaborative behavior contract with clear expectations, rewards, and consequences that involve the student

Explanation: Behavior contracts are most effective when developed collaboratively with clear expectations, rewards, and consequences. Involving the student in this process helps ensure that the contract is meaningful and motivating.

103. What is the role of functional communication training (FCT) in supporting students with communication disorders?

A) To ignore communication needs and focus solely on academic instruction
B) To teach students alternative ways to communicate their needs and desires effectively
C) To limit communication to non-verbal methods only
D) To focus only on improving verbal speech without other communication supports

Answer: B) To teach students alternative ways to communicate their needs and desires effectively

Explanation: Functional Communication Training (FCT) helps students with communication disorders by teaching them alternative ways to communicate their needs and desires effectively. This approach improves their ability to interact and participate in various settings.

104. How can teachers use cooperative learning to support students with special needs?

A) Encouraging only individual work without peer interaction
B) Implementing cooperative learning activities that promote collaboration and provide peer support
C) Limiting group work and focusing solely on independent tasks
D) Ignoring the need for collaborative activities in favor of lecture-based instruction

Answer: B) Implementing cooperative learning activities that promote collaboration and provide peer support

Explanation: Cooperative learning supports students with special needs by promoting collaboration and providing peer support. These activities encourage students to work together, share knowledge, and support each other's learning.

105. What is an effective way to support students with fine motor difficulties in completing written tasks?

A) Using only traditional writing tools and methods
B) Providing alternative tools such as adaptive keyboards, writing aids, and typing software
C) Ignoring fine motor needs and expecting students to use standard writing methods
D) Limiting written tasks to simple sentences only

Answer: B) Providing alternative tools such as adaptive keyboards, writing aids, and typing software

Explanation: Supporting students with fine motor difficulties involves providing alternative tools such as adaptive keyboards, writing aids, and typing software. These tools help students complete written tasks more effectively.

106. How can teachers use social stories to support students with Autism Spectrum Disorder (ASD)?

A) Providing only verbal instructions for social situations
B) Using social stories to help students understand and navigate social interactions and expectations
C) Ignoring the need for social stories and focusing solely on behavioral management
D) Using social stories only for academic content

Answer: B) Using social stories to help students understand and navigate social interactions and expectations

Explanation: Social stories are used to help students with ASD understand and navigate social interactions and expectations. They provide clear, visual explanations of social situations and appropriate responses.

107. What is a key principle of providing effective feedback to students with special needs?

A) Offering vague and general comments
B) Providing specific, constructive feedback that highlights strengths and areas for improvement
C) Ignoring feedback and focusing only on grades
D) Giving feedback only at the end of a grading period

Answer: B) Providing specific, constructive feedback that highlights strengths and areas for improvement

Explanation: Effective feedback for students with special needs should be specific and constructive, highlighting both strengths and areas for improvement. This approach helps students understand their progress and areas that need further development.

108. How can teachers support students with special needs in participating in extracurricular activities?

A) Limiting participation to only academic activities
B) Encouraging and providing support for students to participate in extracurricular activities based on their interests and abilities
C) Ignoring the need for extracurricular involvement and focusing only on academics
D) Restricting participation to non-inclusive activities

Answer: B) Encouraging and providing support for students to participate in extracurricular activities based on their interests and abilities

Explanation: Supporting students with special needs in participating in extracurricular activities involves encouraging and providing support based on their interests and abilities. This participation helps students develop social skills, confidence, and a sense of belonging.

109. What is an important aspect of designing inclusive physical education activities for students with special needs?

A) Using a one-size-fits-all approach to physical activities
B) Adapting activities to ensure that all students can participate and benefit from the experience
C) Limiting physical activities to those that do not require modifications
D) Ignoring individual needs and focusing solely on competitive sports

Answer: B) Adapting activities to ensure that all students can participate and benefit from the experience

Explanation: Designing inclusive physical education activities involves adapting activities so that all students, including those with special needs, can participate and benefit from the experience. This ensures that physical education is accessible and enjoyable for every student.

110. How can teachers use visual supports to enhance comprehension for students with special needs?

A) Limiting visual supports to decorative purposes
B) Integrating visual supports such as charts, diagrams, and picture cues to clarify and reinforce instruction
C) Ignoring the need for visual supports and relying solely on verbal explanations
D) Using visual supports only for specific subjects

Answer: B) Integrating visual supports such as charts, diagrams, and picture cues to clarify and reinforce instruction

Explanation: Visual supports such as charts, diagrams, and picture cues enhance comprehension by clarifying and reinforcing instruction. They provide additional visual information that helps students with special needs understand and retain content.

111. What is a key factor in creating an effective Individualized Education Program (IEP) meeting?

A) Conducting meetings without input from the student and their family
B) Collaborating with the student, family, and other team members to develop a comprehensive and personalized plan
C) Focusing solely on administrative aspects of the IEP
D) Limiting discussions to only academic goals

Answer: B) Collaborating with the student, family, and other team members to develop a comprehensive and personalized plan

Explanation: An effective IEP meeting involves collaborating with the student, family, and other team members to develop a comprehensive and personalized plan. This teamwork ensures that the IEP addresses the student's unique needs and sets achievable goals.

112. How can teachers support students with ADHD in managing classroom tasks?

A) Ignoring organizational needs and focusing solely on task completion
B) Providing organizational tools, clear instructions, and regular check-ins to help students manage tasks effectively
C) Limiting supports to only individual tasks
D) Using punitive measures to address task management issues

Answer: B) Providing organizational tools, clear instructions, and regular check-ins to help students manage tasks effectively

Explanation: Supporting students with ADHD involves providing organizational tools, clear instructions, and regular check-ins. These strategies help students manage their tasks and stay focused in the classroom.

113. What is a primary benefit of using role-playing activities for students with special needs?

A) Providing only individual work opportunities
B) Offering a chance to practice and develop social and communication skills in a structured setting
C) Limiting role-playing to academic content only
D) Ignoring the need for social skill development

Answer: B) Offering a chance to practice and develop social and communication skills in a structured setting

Explanation: Role-playing activities provide students with special needs an opportunity to practice and develop social and communication skills in a structured setting. This practice helps students navigate social interactions and improve their social competence.

114. How can teachers ensure that accommodations for students with special needs are implemented effectively?

A) Providing accommodations without monitoring their effectiveness
B) Regularly reviewing and adjusting accommodations based on student progress and feedback
C) Ignoring student feedback and using fixed accommodations
D) Implementing accommodations only for specific assignments

Answer: B) Regularly reviewing and adjusting accommodations based on student progress and feedback

Explanation: To ensure accommodations are effective, teachers should regularly review and adjust them based on student progress and feedback. This ongoing evaluation helps ensure that accommodations continue to meet the student's needs.

115. What is an important consideration when using behavior charts to support students with special needs?

A) Creating a chart with no input from the student
B) Designing behavior charts that are clear, achievable, and involve the student in setting goals
C) Using behavior charts only for academic behaviors
D) Ignoring student input and focusing solely on teacher-set goals

Answer: B) Designing behavior charts that are clear, achievable, and involve the student in setting goals

Explanation: Effective behavior charts should be clear, achievable, and involve the student in setting goals. This approach helps ensure that the charts are meaningful and motivating for the student.

116. How can teachers use technology to support students with special needs in accessing the curriculum?

A) Limiting technology use to only non-educational purposes
B) Integrating educational technology tools such as interactive apps, audiobooks, and adaptive software to enhance learning
C) Ignoring the potential benefits of technology and using traditional methods only
D) Providing technology without considering individual needs and preferences

Answer: B) Integrating educational technology tools such as interactive apps, audiobooks, and adaptive software to enhance learning

Explanation: Integrating educational technology tools, such as interactive apps, audiobooks, and adaptive software, supports students with special needs in accessing the curriculum. These tools can enhance learning and provide alternative ways to engage with content.

117. What is a key strategy for supporting students with communication disorders in group activities?

A) Limiting group interactions and focusing solely on individual tasks
B) Providing supports such as communication devices, peer assistance, and clear instructions to facilitate participation
C) Ignoring communication needs and expecting students to manage independently
D) Using only verbal communication without considering alternative methods

Answer: B) Providing supports such as communication devices, peer assistance, and clear instructions to facilitate participation

Explanation: Supporting students with communication disorders in group activities involves providing supports such as communication devices, peer assistance, and clear instructions. These strategies facilitate participation and ensure that students can contribute effectively.

118. How can teachers address the needs of students with sensory processing disorders in the classroom?

A) Ignoring sensory needs and using a standard classroom setup
B) Creating a sensory-friendly environment with options for sensory breaks and calming tools
C) Limiting sensory supports to specific activities
D) Using only verbal instructions without considering sensory sensitivities

Answer: B) Creating a sensory-friendly environment with options for sensory breaks and calming tools

Explanation: Addressing the needs of students with sensory processing disorders involves creating a sensory-friendly environment with options for sensory breaks and calming tools. These accommodations help students manage sensory sensitivities and participate more effectively in classroom activities.

119. What is an important aspect of providing effective instructional feedback to students with special needs?

A) Giving feedback only at the end of the term
B) Offering timely, specific, and actionable feedback that guides students on how to improve
C) Providing vague comments without guidance
D) Focusing only on summative assessments for feedback

Answer: B) Offering timely, specific, and actionable feedback that guides students on how to improve

Explanation: Effective instructional feedback should be timely, specific, and actionable. This type of feedback helps students understand their progress, identify areas for improvement, and make necessary adjustments to their learning strategies.

120. How can teachers support students with special needs in developing self-advocacy skills?

A) Ignoring the need for self-advocacy and focusing solely on instruction
B) Teaching students to understand their strengths, needs, and how to communicate their needs effectively
C) Limiting opportunities for students to practice self-advocacy skills
D) Providing no guidance on self-advocacy and focusing only on academic content

Answer: B) Teaching students to understand their strengths, needs, and how to communicate their needs effectively

Explanation: Supporting students in developing self-advocacy skills involves teaching them to understand their strengths and needs and how to communicate these effectively. This helps students become more independent and assertive in advocating for their own learning needs.

121. How can teachers effectively use collaborative strategies to support students with special needs?

A) Limiting collaboration to teacher-led activities only
B) Implementing collaborative strategies such as peer support, group work, and team-based projects to enhance learning
C) Focusing solely on individual tasks without collaborative opportunities
D) Ignoring the benefits of collaboration and relying only on direct instruction

Answer: B) Implementing collaborative strategies such as peer support, group work, and team-based projects to enhance learning

Explanation: Collaborative strategies such as peer support, group work, and team-based projects enhance learning by providing students with special needs opportunities to work together and support each other. These strategies foster social interaction and shared learning experiences.

122. What is a key component of creating a positive classroom culture for students with special needs?

A) Focusing only on academic performance without considering social dynamics
B) Establishing a welcoming environment that promotes respect, inclusivity, and mutual support
C) Ignoring the need for a positive culture and focusing solely on behavioral management
D) Limiting opportunities for student interaction and collaboration

Answer: B) Establishing a welcoming environment that promotes respect, inclusivity, and mutual support

Explanation: A positive classroom culture for students with special needs involves establishing a welcoming environment that promotes respect, inclusivity, and mutual support. This type of culture helps students feel valued and supported, enhancing their overall learning experience.

123. How can teachers support students with special needs in developing problem-solving skills?

A) Providing solutions without encouraging independent thinking
B) Offering opportunities for students to engage in problem-solving activities and guiding them through the process
C) Ignoring problem-solving needs and focusing solely on rote memorization
D) Limiting problem-solving activities to specific subjects only

Answer: B) Offering opportunities for students to engage in problem-solving activities and guiding them through the process

Explanation: Supporting students in developing problem-solving skills involves providing opportunities for them to engage in problem-solving activities and guiding them through the process. This approach helps students develop critical thinking and decision-making abilities.

124. What is an important consideration when using assistive technology with students who have physical disabilities?

A) Providing technology that is not user-friendly or accessible
B) Selecting assistive technology that is tailored to the student's specific physical needs and abilities
C) Ignoring the need for assistive technology and using standard classroom tools
D) Limiting technology use to only academic subjects

Answer: B) Selecting assistive technology that is tailored to the student's specific physical needs and abilities

Explanation: When using assistive technology with students who have physical disabilities, it is important to select technology that is tailored to the student's specific physical needs and abilities. This ensures that the technology effectively supports the student's learning and participation.

125. How can teachers incorporate student interests into lesson planning for students with special needs?

A) Ignoring student interests and focusing only on standard curriculum
B) Integrating student interests into lesson plans to increase engagement and motivation
C) Limiting lesson plans to only academic content without considering student interests
D) Providing a fixed curriculum without room for adjustments based on interests

Answer: B) Integrating student interests into lesson plans to increase engagement and motivation

Explanation: Incorporating student interests into lesson planning helps increase engagement and motivation. When students see connections between their interests and the curriculum, they are more likely to be engaged and invested in their learning.

126. What is a key strategy for supporting students with special needs in developing organizational skills?

A) Ignoring organizational needs and focusing only on academic content
B) Providing tools and strategies such as planners, visual schedules, and organizational aids
C) Limiting organizational supports to specific subjects only
D) Focusing solely on independent work without guidance

Answer: B) Providing tools and strategies such as planners, visual schedules, and organizational aids

Explanation: Supporting students with special needs in developing organizational skills involves providing tools and strategies like planners, visual schedules, and organizational aids. These supports help students manage their tasks and stay organized effectively.

127. How can teachers create a supportive environment for students with emotional and behavioral disorders?

A) Ignoring emotional and behavioral needs and focusing solely on academic instruction
B) Implementing strategies such as positive behavior support, emotional regulation techniques, and providing a safe space for students to express their feelings
C) Limiting supports to academic content only
D) Using punitive measures to address emotional and behavioral challenges

Answer: B) Implementing strategies such as positive behavior support, emotional regulation techniques, and providing a safe space for students to express their feelings

Explanation: Creating a supportive environment for students with emotional and behavioral disorders involves implementing strategies such as positive behavior support, emotional regulation techniques, and providing a safe space for students to express their feelings. These approaches help address emotional and behavioral needs effectively.

128. What is an important consideration when setting academic goals for students with special needs?

A) Setting goals that are too challenging and unrealistic
B) Establishing goals that are specific, achievable, and aligned with the student's individual needs and abilities
C) Ignoring individual needs and setting generic goals for all students
D) Focusing solely on long-term goals without considering short-term objectives

Answer: B) Establishing goals that are specific, achievable, and aligned with the student's individual needs and abilities

Explanation: Setting academic goals for students with special needs involves establishing goals that are specific, achievable, and aligned with the student's individual needs and abilities. This ensures that goals are realistic and tailored to the student's unique learning profile.

129. How can teachers support students with special needs in transitioning between activities or settings?

A) Providing no support and expecting students to transition independently
B) Offering clear, consistent cues and preparing students in advance for transitions between activities or settings
C) Ignoring transition needs and focusing solely on instructional content
D) Limiting transitions to only academic settings

Answer: B) Offering clear, consistent cues and preparing students in advance for transitions between activities or settings

Explanation: Supporting students with special needs during transitions involves offering clear, consistent cues and preparing students in advance. This helps students understand and manage changes between activities or settings, reducing anxiety and promoting smoother transitions.

130. What is a key principle of differentiated instruction for students with special needs?

A) Using a single instructional approach for all students
B) Adapting instruction to meet the diverse needs of students by providing multiple ways to access content and demonstrate understanding
C) Ignoring individual differences and focusing only on one method of instruction
D) Limiting differentiation to only a few students

Answer: B) Adapting instruction to meet the diverse needs of students by providing multiple ways to access content and demonstrate understanding

Explanation: Differentiated instruction involves adapting teaching methods and materials to meet the diverse needs of students. By providing multiple ways to access content and demonstrate understanding, teachers ensure that all students have equitable opportunities to learn and succeed.

131. How can teachers effectively support students with special needs in developing social skills?

A) Ignoring social skill development and focusing only on academic content
B) Using structured social skills training, role-playing activities, and peer interactions to teach and reinforce social skills
C) Limiting social skill instruction to specific subjects
D) Providing only verbal instructions without opportunities for practice

Answer: B) Using structured social skills training, role-playing activities, and peer interactions to teach and reinforce social skills

Explanation: Supporting students with special needs in developing social skills involves using structured social skills training, role-playing activities, and peer interactions. These methods help students practice and reinforce their social skills in various contexts.

132. What is a primary benefit of using a multi-sensory approach in teaching students with special needs?

A) Limiting instruction to only one sensory modality
B) Engaging multiple senses to enhance learning and accommodate different learning styles
C) Ignoring sensory preferences and focusing solely on verbal instruction
D) Providing only visual aids without considering other sensory modalities

Answer: B) Engaging multiple senses to enhance learning and accommodate different learning styles

Explanation: A multi-sensory approach engages multiple senses to enhance learning and accommodate different learning styles. This approach helps students with special needs by providing various ways to interact with and understand content.

133. How can teachers support students with special needs in developing self-regulation skills?

A) Providing no guidance on self-regulation and focusing solely on academic content
B) Teaching and modeling self-regulation techniques such as mindfulness, coping strategies, and emotional management
C) Ignoring self-regulation needs and relying only on behavioral management strategies
D) Limiting self-regulation support to specific subjects

Answer: B) Teaching and modeling self-regulation techniques such as mindfulness, coping strategies, and emotional management

Explanation: Supporting students with special needs in developing self-regulation skills involves teaching and modeling techniques such as mindfulness, coping strategies, and emotional management. These skills help students manage their emotions and behavior more effectively.

134. What is an important consideration when creating a classroom environment for students with special needs?

A) Using a rigid, unchanging environment for all students
B) Designing a flexible and adaptable environment that meets the diverse needs of students with special needs
C) Ignoring individual needs and using a standard classroom setup
D) Limiting environmental changes to only a few areas

Answer: B) Designing a flexible and adaptable environment that meets the diverse needs of students with special needs

Explanation: Creating a classroom environment for students with special needs involves designing a flexible and adaptable space that meets diverse needs. This approach helps accommodate different learning styles and supports various accessibility requirements.

135. How can teachers support students with special needs in developing independence?

A) Providing constant supervision and support without opportunities for independent work
B) Encouraging and providing opportunities for students to take on tasks independently while offering guidance and support as needed
C) Limiting independent tasks and focusing only on guided activities
D) Ignoring the need for independence and focusing solely on teacher-led instruction

Answer: B) Encouraging and providing opportunities for students to take on tasks independently while offering guidance and support as needed

Explanation: Supporting students with special needs in developing independence involves encouraging them to take on tasks independently while offering guidance and support as needed. This approach helps students build confidence and self-reliance.

136. What is a key consideration when providing academic accommodations for students with special needs?

A) Using a one-size-fits-all approach to accommodations
B) Tailoring accommodations to address the specific needs of each student and ensuring they are implemented effectively
C) Ignoring individual needs and providing generic accommodations
D) Limiting accommodations to only academic subjects

Answer: B) Tailoring accommodations to address the specific needs of each student and ensuring they are implemented effectively

Explanation: Academic accommodations should be tailored to address the specific needs of each student and implemented effectively. This personalized approach ensures that accommodations are meaningful and supportive for the student's learning needs.

137. How can teachers support students with special needs in developing problem-solving skills?

A) Providing solutions without encouraging independent thinking
B) Offering opportunities for students to engage in problem-solving activities and guiding them through the process
C) Ignoring problem-solving needs and focusing solely on rote memorization
D) Limiting problem-solving activities to specific subjects only

Answer: B) Offering opportunities for students to engage in problem-solving activities and guiding them through the process

Explanation: Supporting students in developing problem-solving skills involves offering opportunities for them to engage in problem-solving activities and guiding them through the process. This approach helps students develop critical thinking and decision-making abilities.

138. How can teachers effectively use peer tutoring to support students with special needs?

A) Limiting peer tutoring to only advanced students
B) Implementing peer tutoring with clear roles, training, and monitoring to ensure effective support for students with special needs
C) Ignoring peer tutoring and focusing solely on teacher-led instruction
D) Providing no guidance on peer tutoring and allowing it to be unstructured

Answer: B) Implementing peer tutoring with clear roles, training, and monitoring to ensure effective support for students with special needs

Explanation: Effective peer tutoring involves clear roles, training, and monitoring to ensure that students with special needs receive appropriate support. This structured approach helps maximize the benefits of peer tutoring.

139. What is an important consideration when providing transition planning for students with special needs?

A) Focusing only on immediate academic goals without considering long-term planning
B) Developing a comprehensive transition plan that includes academic, social, and vocational goals to support a successful transition to adulthood
C) Ignoring long-term goals and focusing solely on short-term academic achievements
D) Limiting transition planning to only academic transitions

Answer: B) Developing a comprehensive transition plan that includes academic, social, and vocational goals to support a successful transition to adulthood

Explanation: Transition planning for students with special needs should be comprehensive, including academic, social, and vocational goals. This holistic approach supports a successful transition to adulthood and helps students prepare for various aspects of life beyond school.

140. How can teachers use student data to inform instruction for students with special needs?

A) Ignoring student data and relying solely on anecdotal observations
B) Analyzing student data to identify strengths, needs, and progress, and using this information to adjust instruction and support
C) Focusing only on data from standardized tests without considering other sources of information
D) Using student data only for grading purposes

Answer: B) Analyzing student data to identify strengths, needs, and progress, and using this information to adjust instruction and support

Explanation: Using student data effectively involves analyzing it to identify strengths, needs, and progress. This information helps teachers adjust instruction and support to better meet the needs of students with special needs.

141. What is an effective strategy for integrating students with special needs into mainstream classrooms?

A) Isolating students with special needs from their peers
B) Providing individualized supports and modifications while promoting interaction with peers
C) Limiting interaction with mainstream students to prevent distractions
D) Focusing solely on special education settings without mainstream integration

Answer: B) Providing individualized supports and modifications while promoting interaction with peers

Explanation: Effective integration involves providing individualized supports and modifications while promoting interaction with peers. This approach helps students with special needs benefit from the general education environment while receiving the necessary supports.

142. How can teachers assess the effectiveness of instructional interventions for students with special needs?

A) Relying solely on informal observations
B) Using a combination of formative assessments, progress monitoring, and student feedback to evaluate intervention effectiveness

C) Focusing only on standardized test results
D) Ignoring data and relying on anecdotal evidence alone

Answer: B) Using a combination of formative assessments, progress monitoring, and student feedback to evaluate intervention effectiveness

Explanation: Assessing the effectiveness of instructional interventions involves using formative assessments, progress monitoring, and student feedback. This comprehensive approach provides a clear picture of how well interventions are working and helps guide adjustments.

143. What is a key consideration when developing individualized education programs (IEPs) for students with special needs?

A) Using a generic template without personalization
B) Developing IEPs that are tailored to the specific needs, strengths, and goals of each student
C) Focusing only on academic goals without considering social and behavioral needs
D) Limiting input from parents and other professionals

Answer: B) Developing IEPs that are tailored to the specific needs, strengths, and goals of each student

Explanation: Individualized Education Programs (IEPs) should be tailored to each student's specific needs, strengths, and goals. This personalization ensures that the IEP addresses the unique aspects of each student's learning profile and supports their overall development.

144. How can teachers support students with special needs in improving their executive functioning skills?

A) Ignoring executive functioning needs and focusing solely on academic content
B) Providing explicit instruction and practice in organization, planning, and time management skills
C) Limiting support to specific subjects only
D) Using only verbal instructions without practical application

Answer: B) Providing explicit instruction and practice in organization, planning, and time management skills

Explanation: Supporting executive functioning skills involves providing explicit instruction and practice in organization, planning, and time management. These skills are crucial for students with special needs to manage their academic and personal responsibilities effectively.

145. What role do positive behavioral interventions and supports (PBIS) play in special education?

A) Ignoring behavioral needs and focusing solely on academic instruction
B) Providing a framework for promoting positive behavior through proactive strategies and support systems
C) Using only punitive measures to address behavioral issues
D) Limiting behavioral support to specific students only

Answer: B) Providing a framework for promoting positive behavior through proactive strategies and support systems

Explanation: Positive Behavioral Interventions and Supports (PBIS) provide a framework for promoting positive behavior through proactive strategies and support systems. This approach helps create a supportive environment that encourages positive behavior and reduces disruptions.

146. How can teachers effectively use visual supports to assist students with special needs?

A) Ignoring visual supports and relying solely on verbal instructions
B) Incorporating visual supports such as charts, schedules, and graphic organizers to enhance understanding and organization
C) Limiting visual supports to specific subjects
D) Providing visual supports without considering individual student needs

Answer: B) Incorporating visual supports such as charts, schedules, and graphic organizers to enhance understanding and organization

Explanation: Visual supports, such as charts, schedules, and graphic organizers, help enhance understanding and organization for students with special needs. These tools provide visual cues that support learning and help students manage tasks and routines.

147. What is a crucial aspect of fostering an inclusive classroom environment for students with special needs?

A) Isolating students with special needs from their peers
B) Promoting inclusivity by encouraging collaboration, respect, and mutual support among all students
C) Limiting interactions between students with special needs and their peers
D) Focusing only on the needs of students with special needs without considering the whole class

Answer: B) Promoting inclusivity by encouraging collaboration, respect, and mutual support among all students

Explanation: Fostering an inclusive classroom environment involves promoting collaboration, respect, and mutual support among all students. This approach helps create a positive atmosphere where every student feels valued and included.

148. How can teachers use formative assessment to support students with special needs?

A) Relying only on summative assessments to evaluate student progress
B) Utilizing formative assessments to provide ongoing feedback and adjust instruction based on students' needs
C) Ignoring formative assessments and focusing solely on standardized tests
D) Providing feedback only at the end of the term

Answer: B) Utilizing formative assessments to provide ongoing feedback and adjust instruction based on students' needs

Explanation: Formative assessments provide ongoing feedback and allow teachers to adjust instruction based on students' needs. This continuous evaluation helps teachers address challenges early and tailor their teaching to better support student learning.

149. What is an effective strategy for teaching students with special needs to self-monitor their progress?

A) Providing no guidance on self-monitoring and focusing only on teacher-led instruction
B) Teaching students how to use tools and techniques for tracking their own progress and setting goals
C) Ignoring self-monitoring and relying solely on teacher assessments
D) Limiting self-monitoring to only specific subjects

Answer: B) Teaching students how to use tools and techniques for tracking their own progress and setting goals

Explanation: Teaching students to self-monitor their progress involves providing tools and techniques for tracking their own learning and setting goals. This helps students develop independence and become more engaged in their own educational progress.

150. How can teachers support students with special needs in developing social-emotional skills?

A) Ignoring social-emotional needs and focusing solely on academics
B) Incorporating social-emotional learning activities, such as role-playing and discussions, into the curriculum
C) Limiting social-emotional learning to specific times or subjects
D) Providing no structured opportunities for social-emotional skill development

Answer: B) Incorporating social-emotional learning activities, such as role-playing and discussions, into the curriculum

Explanation: Supporting social-emotional skill development involves incorporating activities such as role-playing and discussions into the curriculum. These activities help students practice and enhance their social-emotional skills in a structured manner.

Made in the USA
Las Vegas, NV
19 September 2024

95478363R00044